Plug-in to

Life

Strategies and Resources for Catholic Youth Ministry from **LIFE TEEN**

Plug-in to Life

Father Dale Fushek

Phil Baniewicz

Tom Booth

and the National Staff of the LIFE TEEN Program

AVE MARIA PRESS   Notre Dame, Indiana 46556

Father Dale Fushek is the pastor of St. Timothy's Church in Mesa, Arizona, and a national leader in the field of youth ministry and a winner of the Pope Paul VI award for evangelization. Based on his belief that the Church should do everything it can to make young people feel loved, he founded the LIFE TEEN program for teens in 1985 at St. Timothy's. In the years since, LIFE TEEN has expanded to hundreds of parishes worldwide.

Phil Baniewicz helped found the LIFE TEEN program. He has worked in the field of youth ministry since 1984 and is currently the executive director of LIFE TEEN. In addition to his work with LIFE TEEN, he also produces television programs and videos and coaches a state championship high school baseball team.

Tom Booth has been the LIFE TEEN music director since 1985. He has eight recordings of his own, and has collaborated with several other Christian musical artists. His music has been very influential in drawing teens to the Church. In 1997, Booth was nominated for "Song of the Year" by the Gospel Music Association. His music is published nationally by Oregon Catholic Press.

Nihil Obstat: Reverend Paul Orel
                     Censor

Imprimatur: The Most Reverend Thomas J. O'Brien,
                     Bishop of Phoenix

Given at Phoenix, AZ on 25 September 1997

The *Imprimatur* is an official declaration that a book or pamphlet is free of doctrinal or moral error. No implication is contained therein that those who have granted the *Imprimatur* agree with its contents, opinions, or statements expressed.

This manual is intended as an introduction and overview of the national *LIFE TEEN Program*®. The material in this manual may be used in any program for teens. However, *LIFE TEEN* is a registered trademark of Catholic Life Incorporated, and use of its name is restricted to programs registered with the national *LIFE TEEN* office. For more information on *LIFE TEEN* please write Catholic Life Incorporated at 1730 West Guadalupe Road, Mesa, AZ, 85202 or call 602-820-7001.

© 1998 by Ave Maria Press, Inc.

International Standard Book Number: 0-87793-644-7

Project Editor: Michael Amodei

Cover and text design by Brian C. Conley

Printed and bound in the United States of America.

Opening Statement

This book provides both an *invitation* to explore the different

components of the LIFE TEEN program and an *explanation* of why

and how this teen ministry has captured the attention of many

parishes throughout North America.

Table of Contents

Introduction:
Setting a Vision of
Teen Ministry

Where Teens Are Today

By Father Dale Fushek

Where are teens today?

Some are at the mall.

Some are at school.

Some are at home with their families.

Some are in the expensive new car that Mommy and Daddy bought for them.

Some are on the football field.

Teens are all over the place.

Few teens, however, are at church.

It's impossible to write an accurate profile of today's teens. The term *teen* itself is a very generic one. Usually it refers to high school students in grades nine through twelve. Yet, teens are not generic people.

Teens are very autonomous. Teens have a multiplicity of backgrounds and tastes.

This information may be surprising to many adults because they always see teens in groups. Teens are thought of as kinds of "pack animals" who always want and need to be with their friends.

But, despite this outward tendency, on the inside teens are struggling to find themselves. They get into "packs" or groups to find security.

Some teens will hang out with druggies.

Some will find a group of jocks.

Others will find a sixties-like hippie crowd.

Still others will hook up with computer nerds.

Teens will look for groups because they do not know themselves, trust themselves, or accept themselves.

The teen years are hard, hard years. This is a change from the Happy Days-type atmosphere many adults experienced a generation ago. Family break-ups, money (too much or too little), sexual promiscuity, gangs, poor educational systems, and an overall decline in moral guidelines and values are some of the reasons for the changes.

When I was in high school, a lot of us thought we were on the edge because we chewed gum in class or sneaked off campus for lunch at a fast food restaurant.

Nowadays, for many youth, being on the edge means carrying a gun to school.

The decisions faced by high school teens today, and the lasting impact these decisions have on these young lives, are overwhelming. The stress and pressure on teens are draining, especially when they have been given few tools to cope with this difficult life.

Many experts say that the root of today's problems is in the family. Because of the break-up of so many families, our young people have no shepherds. I am always moved when I am on a high school campus. The words of Jesus, "They are like sheep without a shepherd" come to life. A great number of teens have no fathers living at home. Some have several "fathers." Some have two homes with two sets of brothers and sisters, and at least two different sets of rules, depending on the day of the week or where they are. Most teens have moms who work outside the home.

Most teens rarely, if ever, sit down for a family dinner. Grandparents and other extended family members usually do not live nearby and other potential adult role models that could come from Church or school are often non-existent.

In general, our teens are disconnected.

This maze of problems has led to the situation we face today: many, many teenagers are out of control.

It's almost like a novice pilot trying to fly a plane when the headset linked to the tower goes out. Maybe the person will be able to continue flying the plane and even land it. But, if that happens, it is a miracle. In other words, most of our teens have little chance of capably handling the pressures of today. It's really a miracle that they come out of these teenage years alive: emotionally, intellectually, spiritually and physically.

As a result of this situation, many teens drink. As a matter of fact, a majority of teens use alcohol. The use of marijuana and other drugs is also on the increase. And it's no longer just the stereotypical druggies using pot. Athletes and honor students alike can be found smoking pot before they go to school as a way to escape the reality of the day.

Statistics also indicate that nearly fifty percent of high school students are also sexually active. Why? I believe teens are seeking some kind of connection with another person. What they are really searching for is an emotional connection, and a sexual encounter seems to them like the best way to find it.

School, for many teens, is something that is only tolerated. They plan to go to college, but they don't plan *for* college, academically or financially. College is just another thing teens feel they are owed. School, government, parents, and even the Church are viewed as organizations that *owe* them something.

All in all, the youth culture that is typified by the media is a sorry culture.

However, within this culture are many good kids who choose to find another path.

For teachers, youth ministers, and parents, these teens are a beacon of light.

These are teens who seek maturity and integrity.

There are teens like these in every school and every parish.

By the way, the other kids are not "bad" kids.

They simply have not been given the chance or do not have the courage to use high school as a time "to grow in age or wisdom."

As Church, we need to understand that we have not helped counteract the situation of the prevalent teen culture.

Most parishes do not have youth programs.

Since the death of the CYO and CCD eras, we have been O-U-T of it with our youth.

The Church needs to do more to support families and marriages. We say we believe in those things, but we haven't acted on them at the parish level.

None of us wants teens to drink, do drugs, join gangs, or commit suicide. We just have failed to put our resources and our best talent to the task of serving our youth. Rather than being a light, we have added to the darkness.

Instead, what can we bring to teens as Church?

A lot.

We have the revealed truth of God, unchangeable truths.

We have a value system, based in natural law, that is written in each of our hearts.

We have the sacraments, great experiences of belonging.

We have the eucharist of God, which can transform hearts.

We have the many graces of the Holy Spirit.

The Church is the one institution, the one presence that can be the guide for our youth.

The pope has tried.

Pope John Paul II has reached far beyond his role as leader of the Church to become the primary youth minister of the Church. Praise God that he has. But also realize what a statement this makes. Local parishes are not reaching their own teens. Not enough is being done to minister to teenagers.

As a result of our lack of youth services, teens believe that we do not care about them.

Instead of seeing the Church as a place to look for the meaning of life in this world and the next, they believe we are old fashioned and out of touch. Though the contrary is true, we need to prove it to our youth. Teens have a built-in respect for the Church, the priesthood, the commandments, and the sacraments. They simply do not see how it affects their daily lives.

LIFE TEEN was created to begin to deal with teens' disconnection from family and Church and our disconnection from them.

Through the sacraments—especially the Eucharist—and through solid, 100 percent Catholic teaching, we are telling teens that we do not think they are irrelevant.

Like the rich young man in the gospels who walked away from Jesus, teens may always reject what we have to say.

That is part of human nature and especially of being young.

But that does not excuse us of our responsibility to share the gospel message with them.

And, it is my belief that once teens hear the gospel, most will accept it. The scriptures do not tell of many others who left Jesus.

After all, teenagers are human beings who are created in the image and likeness of Jesus. Their hearts were created to know and love God.

We just need to reach them.

Understanding Youth Ministry

Teen Culture

Only through understanding contemporary teen culture can adults be expected to reach teens effectively. The youth culture includes but is not limited to:

- teen language (being able to decipher phrases and clichés)
- teen clothing
- the media teens like (movies, music, television, Internet activities)
- teen cliques (including gangs)
- places teens hang out

Understanding these elements of teen culture can help adults to key into deeper attitudes and beliefs of teens. They provide a window to chart what's going on inside the heart, soul, and mind of teens.

Issues Affecting Teens Today

Author Merton Strommen's book *The Five Cries of Youth* dissected five of the most important issues affecting teens today. Understanding these issues is essential for those who minister to teens. LIFE TEEN has adapted some of these to apply to today's teens. These issues—the "cries of youth"—are the following:

1. Loneliness. Even though many teens spend a great amount of time in large groups, they actually feel an inner isolation. Teens attempt to rid themselves of loneliness in many inappropriate ways: through sexual activity, drug use, alcoholism, gang membership, and other dangerous activities related to peer pressure.

2. Self-image/Self-hatred. In spite of various outward appearances and actions, teens do not like who they are. Teens are not aware of how much God loves them.

3. Family. Family issues bother teens a great deal. Broken relationships with parents or siblings cause teens great pain. Multiply this in situations (upwards of 50 percent) when families are broken by divorce, separation, and death, and the problem is quite staggering.

4. Fear of commitment. Teenagers have a hard time committing to anything. They are always waiting for "something better to come along." Commitment to Jesus Christ is especially difficult.

5. Joy. Teens do not know healthy ways to express joy. Violence, drug use, and sexual activity often form part of the landscape celebrating events like proms, games, and graduations.

Sr. Mary Rose McCready, the national director of Covenant House, also adds insight into key issues affecting teens. McCready names and describes them in the following ways:

- Teens are isolated. With both parents working in most families, there is little chance for interaction among children and Mom and Dad. The media, culture, and peers exert more influence and often carry more respect among teens than parents.

- There is a sense of hopelessness among youth. The hopelessness is so acute that teens have become numb to moral atrocities of the worst kinds (violence, murder, suicide) and are turning themselves off emotionally.

"Stay in the teen culture to know what is going on with teens, so that you can more effectively minister to them."

—Phil Baniewicz,
Executive Director of LIFE TEEN

The Importance of Youth Ministry

Youth ministry is absolutely essential because it is so closely connected to the mission of the Church. Recall Jesus' final recorded command in the gospel of Matthew: "Go, therefore, and make disciples of all nations, baptizing them in the name of the Father, and of the Son, and of the Holy Spirit, teaching them to observe all that I have commanded you" (28:19).

Baptism literally means to "immerse." The Church's job is to immerse the whole world in Christ. We are not called to immerse *only* adults, *only* children, *only* old people, *only* the sick, or *only* prisoners. "All nations" means everyone. Including teens. In fact, in this day and age, especially teens. Here's why:

First, in recent times, the Church has done a poor job in ministering to youth. This is not meant to criticize or diminish the efforts of many fine diocesan and parish youth ministry programs. But speaking in general terms, the Church's efforts to minister to teens have fallen on deaf ears or failed outright.

In the past, parish youth ministry took the form of the CYO (Catholic Youth Organization). In this model, teens came to the parish for dances, socials, and sports. As they participated in these events, formation took place. The youth took their identity in being Catholic.

Also, the parish CYO efforts were supported by the religious formation most teens received by attending Catholic high schools.

Replacing the CYO in parishes was a classroom model of youth ministry. Simultaneously, a smaller percentage of baptized Catholic teens attended Catholic high schools. Because of this the heart of these new parish programs was in *transmitting* religious content and doctrine to the teens. In general, this model was unsuccessful because religion became solely a "head" matter, and not something of both head and heart. Also, since teens were required to attend by their teachers and parents, bad attitudes developed. Many teens stopped coming altogether.

A second reason that ministry to teens must take primary focus in the Church today is that the pressures on teens today are excessively dangerous. Teens today are at physical, intellectual, emotional, and spiritual risk more than ever before, and they are more at risk than any other age category.

For these reasons, youth ministry must be placed at the top of what is important. Pope John Paul II stresses this message wherever he goes, especially through the holding of World Youth Days. He reminds us that in the youth's search for God, "they cannot help but encounter the Church." Pope John Paul continues:

And the Church also cannot help but encounter the young. The only necessity is that the Church have a profound understanding of what it means to be young, of the importance that youth has for every person. It is also necessary that the young know the Church, that they perceive Christ in the Church, Christ who walks through the centuries alongside each generation, alongside every person.

—(quoted from Crossing the Threshold of Hope, *p. 126)*

Learning From a Back-Row Teen

In Sabrina's freshman year we began the LIFE TEEN program here at St. Mary's. Sabrina immediately stood out as one of the "back-row" teens, that is, one who would talk and socialize at the back of the Church during Mass, not paying attention at all.

Together with her other back-row buddies, Sabrina would leave before Mass. My initial reaction to their departure was "Good! Now we can pray! And thank heavens they won't be around to cause trouble at our LIFE Night." We wouldn't see them again until the following Sunday.

But the Lord put an itch in several of us on the core team, and we began to reach out to Sabrina and her group. We learned of their reputation as heavy partiers, daring and defiant at home, and marginally successful academically. But we also learned how much we liked them, even though they were definitely coming to Mass only because they "had to."

In time, through steady and genuine attention by the core team members, they began to stay through Mass and hang around a bit afterwards as if they were trying to decide whether to give us a try. Finally, the prospect of food won them over and they stayed for a LIFE Night. Their behavior at the LIFE Night was about what we expected: somewhat rowdy, sticking to themselves, hanging toward the back, leaving ahead of time. But over time, they were gradually drawn in. By springtime, we had convinced them to go on retreat with us, about which we were thrilled—and prayerfully concerned.

Several concerns and suspicions of Sabrina and her friends surfaced throughout the retreat weekend. Every break they rushed to the only smoking area we provided. They even smoked in the rain. Fr. Bill spent quite a bit of time standing and talking with them as they smoked. We weren't sure if we were reaching out to them or just chaperoning them.

We learned the truth on the last day of the retreat. All the teens were invited to share their impressions and Sabrina spoke up.

In her heart, she said, she was longing to belong. But, she sensed all of our "reservations and hesitations" about her and all of her fellow back-row buddies. She quoted the gospel and told us that we had the duty to make Christ present to all people, strangers as well as friends, those who are like us and those who are not.

In front of 150 teens and a core team, a brave Sabrina taught us a hard lesson about accepting others not for what they look like, or what they wear, or who they hang with, but for the simple fact that they too are part of the body of Christ.

—Beth Davis
**LIFE TEEN Northeast Regional Consultant
Hudson, Ohio**

Holistic Youth Ministry

Effective youth ministry is holistic, that is it reaches teens on all levels—emotional, intellectual, spiritual, and relational. Some youth ministry programs have spent too much time on one or the other. For example, the classroom model has focused almost exclusively on intellectual goals. Teens are expected to repeat back to adults information given to them.

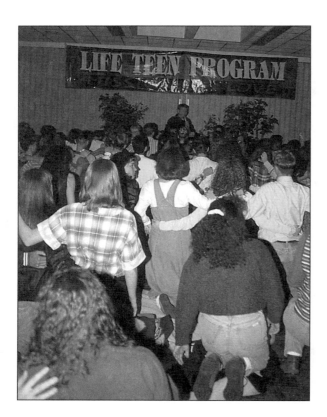

Faith development is more than that. Faith is about the whole being, not only about what you think about, but what you say. It's what you expose your eyes to. It's what you do with your feet. It's how you use your whole being. Being a Catholic is about the whole process. Holistic programs cover every part of our being:

- emotional

- intellectual

- spiritual

- relational

When Jesus was on the earth, he didn't talk about spaceships. Rather, he talked about things that his audience knew about and that mattered to them. Effective youth ministry today does the same. This means that topics of importance to teens—sexuality, AIDS, drug abuse, suicide—must be explored, not ignored.

Goals of Youth Ministry

Youth Ministry Is Transformational

The key to effective youth ministry is to create an environment where transformation can happen. Transformation is different from formation. Formation has to do with how a person thinks or acts and the limits that are set for his or her behavior. Formation is essential for human growth. But in order to make a Christian, transformation has to take place. Transformation is a change of being. A change in the way a person looks at things. A change of heart.

Formation is about a change of behavior; for example, a teen who once got all F's now gets all A's. A teen who did not know the Ten Commandments now has them memorized. Formation is certainly important and elements of it are a part of successful youth ministry.

But transformation is even more important. Transformation happens when your heart changes. Transformation is when you fall so deeply in love with God that you begin to ask God, "How do I live? What do you want from me?" Creating an environment that lends itself to transformation is essential; this most concretely involves centering the teens in the sacraments, especially Eucharist.

Youth Ministry Is Eucharist-Centered

The focus on the sacraments, especially the Eucharist, is necessary for transformation of lives to happen. People change through their experiences. Liturgy is the place where we encounter Christ. The experience of Eucharist changes hearts.

God the Father gives us the flesh and blood of his only Son to enter into our very being and change us. It is not a greeting card; it's the Real Presence. A foundational principle for teen ministry is that everything the teens bring flows *into* the altar, and all subsequent programming flows *from* the altar. If we do that we are creating an environment for conversion to take place, for transformation to happen.

The Mass is the heart of the Catholic faith. Jesus is truly present at Mass. The Mass is where we come together to be with Jesus. A well-done teen Mass allows teens to experience and understand God on their level. It gives teens a sense of identity as Roman Catholics. It provides an opportunity for real and lasting transformation.

So There I Was: At Mass Every Sunday

Born into a non-religious family, my only church experiences as a child were at weddings. During my twelfth-grade year, however, I was exposed for the first time to the Catholic Church and someone named Jesus Christ.

At the time, I was slowly preparing myself for university. I studied relatively hard, and got involved in the student council, the volleyball team, and the music program. I thought I had enough on my plate. So why was Gail, my girlfriend of two years, bugging me to go to church with her every Saturday night? If I wanted preaching and lecture, I thought, I could just stay home and listen to my parents. Nevertheless, I went with Gail to Mass at St. Paul's, half to make her happy, and the other half to get a free dinner with her family after Mass!

Don't get me wrong, I wasn't disrespectful or anything like that. It's just that I had no clue to what was going on, and I didn't pay attention to Gail's good explanations. About the only thing I looked forward to was the sign of peace, where I would become a hand-shaking machine, grabbing every loose hand I could find.

This pattern continued for a year or so. I would go to Mass one week, skip for a couple of weeks, and then maybe go for three straight weeks. I went when it was convenient for me to do so.

I graduated from high school, got accepted to the University of British Columbia's commerce program, and started a full-time job at a trendy Italian restaurant. Soon, a friend of mine named Christina decided to start a new youth choir at St. Paul's to sing at the 9 a.m. Mass. She asked both Gail and me to join her: Gail for her voice, me for moral support, probably. While in the choir, I began to observe more things and to develop an interest in what was happening at Mass. So there I was: at Mass every Sunday. Yet I wasn't even baptized. Can you say RCIA?

My eight-month journey was challenging, yet very rewarding. As Easter got closer and closer, I had a few lingering doubts, but they were quickly shooed away with the assistance of Gail and Christina. Finally the Saturday night Easter vigil came, and it was time to take the next giant step. In one awesome night I was baptized, confirmed, and I received my first communion.

My first few months as a Catholic were exciting. Mass meant so much more to me, and I tried to learn as much as I could every time I stepped into the church. Soon after I received the opportunity of a lifetime: a chance to go to Denver, Colorado, for World Youth Day.

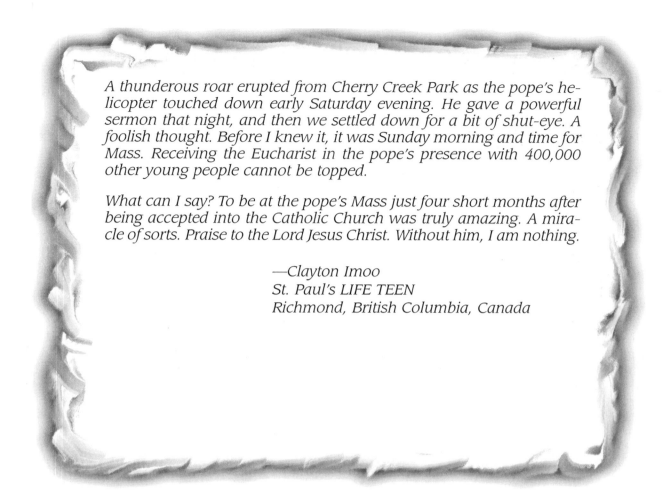

A thunderous roar erupted from Cherry Creek Park as the pope's helicopter touched down early Saturday evening. He gave a powerful sermon that night, and then we settled down for a bit of shut-eye. A foolish thought. Before I knew it, it was Sunday morning and time for Mass. Receiving the Eucharist in the pope's presence with 400,000 other young people cannot be topped.

What can I say? To be at the pope's Mass just four short months after being accepted into the Catholic Church was truly amazing. A miracle of sorts. Praise to the Lord Jesus Christ. Without him, I am nothing.

—Clayton Imoo
St. Paul's LIFE TEEN
Richmond, British Columbia, Canada

Youth Ministry Is Evangelization

One understanding of evangelization is reaching people who have not been baptized, calling them to Christ and to initiation into the Church.

But working with baptized Catholics is evangelization as well, especially those who are unevangelized in terms of really knowing Christ and the good news. Many, if not most, teens fit into this category. Evangelization involves immersing people in Christ. Every good youth ministry program involves evangelization.

Also, liturgy is evangelization. At liturgy, people evangelize one another. By singing God's praises, by sharing God's word, by breaking the bread, by proclaiming one's faith, evangelization takes place.

A saying of the LIFE TEEN program is that "the Mass never ends; it must be lived." When teens are sent forth from Eucharist to share how the experience of God in liturgy has touched their lives with other teens, evangelization, too, is taking place. Every single person is in constant need of being evangelized. And every single person is constantly involved in evangelizing others.

The Experience of Good Liturgy

What Is Liturgy?

There's a weird logic that holds that if something is worth doing, it's worth doing poorly. The underlying assumption is that if something is worth doing and you can't do it well, at least you should do it *somehow.* This seems to be the reasoning supporting the effort of several "teen Masses."

Often a parish advertises a teen Mass and then only puts a teen in sanctuary to do a reading or a few teens near the door to hand out song sheets. These efforts do not make a teen Mass, nor what could be described as good liturgy.

Instead, there are certain liturgical principles that must be followed in order to make good liturgy, be it liturgy with teens, children, or the entire community.

Considering the word *orthodox* is a place to start. Literally, "orthodox" means "to praise rightly." That definition begs the question, "Is it possible to praise God *wrongly?*" The answer is yes.

When false statements are made about God or when liturgy is done that says something untrue about God or God's revelation, then people are praising wrongly. So the Church defines what is orthodox in terms of both its teaching and in terms of liturgy.

What is liturgy? *Liturgy is a public work done for the service of others.* It is public, not private. Liturgy is not meant to be someone's solitary time with God. That would be crazy, for a person to gather in a large church with hundreds of other people only to have private time with God. Liturgy is a very public effort.

Liturgy is also work. Who does the work at liturgy? The priest? Sure, the priest works. But not just the priest. Everyone is charged to do work. Everyone is called to full participation, to sing and respond with everything they have. Just as the priest is there for the people, the people are there for the priest.

By participating in liturgy in this way, by coming together in a public way and by our participation, we make statements about what we believe about God and we build ourselves up.

Usually, this isn't the sense of liturgy that teens have. Teens often feel liturgy is irrelevant.

To change this view, we have to look at liturgy in a new way, or at least in a way that seems new. Actually this view is the charge given to us by the Second Vatican Council over thirty years ago. The council made several strong statements about the liturgy. To ignore them is to ignore a mandate of the Church. Among the statements are:

- *There should be full, conscious, active participation in the liturgy.* "Full" means that everyone should do all they can do. "Active" means that people are actively engaged. "Conscious" means they know what they are doing.

- We are *called to celebrate liturgy with an ever-increasing vigor.* Remember, this is a directive from the ecumenical council. How many Masses do you attend that have this vigor and celebrate it well?

- The *liturgy is the Source and Summit of the life of the Church.* It is the most important thing we do as Church

The Second Vatican Council made changes so that people could be engaged in the liturgy, experience Christ in the sacrament of Eucharist, and have their hearts changed so that they could then change the world. That is why the Council said that (1) the Mass is to be celebrated in the language of the people; (2) the altar is to be moved away from the back wall of the sanctuary; and (3) the presiding priest is to be turned around to face the assembly.

In doing good liturgy for teens, we are trying to reverse a common trend. Instead of teens congregating and remaining in the vestibule, we want to bring them to the front of the church where they can fulfill their mandate to be active participants.

A Vision of Liturgy

According to the scriptures, "Where there is no vision the people perish." In this case, perish is not spelled p-a-r-i-s-h, but in so many parishes people are in fact perishing because liturgy is not being done well. Instead, the Church's vision of liturgy is one in which all people are engaged as full, conscious, and active participants in some of the following ways:

— as a minister of hospitality, everyone is called to be welcoming of others and to be working to maintain a spirit of openness;

— as a minister of the Word, everyone must hear the Word and live the Word;

— as a eucharistic minister, everyone must give and receive the presence of Christ.

A vision of liturgy means acknowledging that Holy Spirit is alive in each person and alive in the community. It is the Holy Spirit who leads us to stand with our brother Jesus in praise of God the Father. Being mindful of this and then incorporating it so that everyone—including teenagers—can participate in full, conscious, and active ways is what good liturgy is about. This is the vision that must come before all liturgy planning and remain with us through the actual celebration of the liturgy itself.

Not the Same Old, Same Old

I love being a priest and I love the liturgy. There is nothing in the world like our Catholic sacramental system. Before LIFE TEEN, I was told that the eucharist was the greatest gift we have as the Church. Unfortunately, it was not what I felt.

All that has changed! From experience, I now know what the Mass can be like, but it has not been easy. We priests need to admit that we sometimes get into a rut in how we celebrate and preside at the Eucharist. Responding to the liturgical and spiritual needs of teenagers has allowed me to be careful not to allow the Mass to slip into the "same old, same old" pattern.

The teens have challenged me out of my comfort zone and I have never regretted it. Celebrating the Mass with teenagers every Sunday evening for the past three years has been one of the greatest gifts God has given me. Because of the LIFE TEEN Mass, I love Eucharist now more than ever before.

The Eucharist is also one of the greatest gifts God has given our teens. When it comes to teens, I like to think of the Mass as a sleeping giant. When it wakes up in a teen's life, it makes a huge difference. Giants do that!

Sadly, for many teens, the giant is still asleep. It needs a little "CPR," that is, Creativity, Passion, and Reverence. If the giant gets it, look out. And, in those programs where the giant has awakened, teens are loving the Eucharist.

Let's wake the giant!
—Fr. Jim McGuinn
Archdiocese of Philadelphia

The Flow of Liturgy

There are four basic elements of a good liturgical flow: gather, break, proclaim, and send. This pattern brings about transformation. These are not only the elements of good liturgy, but of any type of meeting. Here is some background on each of these segments of liturgy.

Gather. The whole idea of liturgy is a public witness we give to the faith. So at the very time a teen (or adult) leaves home, the gathering rite has already begun. It's not something that happens on the first guitar chord. It is a whole sense of hospitality. It has to do with how the church environment is arranged and who is there to offer a greeting. It is crucial that in the gathering time that everyone who comes to church knows that they belong. When you feel welcome, you are ready to participate.

Proclaim. This is the part of the Mass from the first reading through the prayers of the faithful. Teens can take the important role of lector, providing they are well prepared. The readings should be done with passion. This part of Mass also lends itself to opportunities for creativity, especially in the homily. The homily is the time when teens can be addressed specifically. This is the time when teens must come to a real understanding of the readings. There are lots of ways to be creative in the homily, including the use of skits, popular music, and liturgical dance.

Break. Looking at an egg for the first time, you'd never know what was inside of it until you broke it open and it started oozing out. This image can be compared to Eucharist. Having gathered the people and proclaimed the Word, the "break" part of the Mass has to do with discovering the Real Presence of Jesus Christ. Breaking entails opening the gift of Jesus in Eucharist. It includes the eucharistic prayer, rite of communion, and prayer after communion.

Send. The word Mass originates from the Latin *Missa*, meaning "to send." The "sending" part of the liturgy begins when everyone is seated after communion. The announcements are given to all the participants. Teens are addressed in a personal and friendly way during this time and encouraged to attend the meeting that follows immediately after the Mass. A LIFE TEEN tradition is to end with the statement that "The Mass never ends; it must be lived." Though the service has a finish, we are to take literally the call of Mass to go out and be the body of Christ to others for all times.

More Than a Sunday Catholic

Throughout my life, I've been involved in a number of activities. However, I have found none that offer me as much support or personal benefit as LIFE TEEN. I realize this sounds corny or altogether fake. But it's true.

Take the Mass, for example. It's geared toward teenagers. The first and second readings are done by teens, the offering is brought up by teens, and there are teens in the choir. These things help young people like myself to develop a greater understanding of the Mass. It also just helps us to feel more involved.

At the end of every Mass, when most people say "The Mass has ended . . ." we say, "the Mass never ends; it must be lived; so let us go forth in peace to love and serve the Lord." I'd never really thought about it before, but that's a really important phrase. That single statement was part of what inspired me to go and do more than just be a "Sunday Catholic." I now try to think about Christ in everything I do. Not just in things that are convenient for me.

—Casey Elmore, age 15
LIFE TEEN Program of Washington County
Hagerstown, Maryland

The Importance of Music

Music at Liturgy

A University of Notre Dame study revealed that there are two components of liturgy that people are most affected by: the homily and the music.

As good overall liturgy can nourish and foster faith, so, too, with music. Good music can uplift faith. Poor music can weaken a person's faith.

Good music at liturgy provides a "holy sound track" to the Mass. In the gathering, the music must draw the people into the worship experience. During the proclaim part of the Mass, the music itself proclaims God's Word, especially in the responsorial psalm. During the break, the music must help the participants focus on the central mystery of Christ's presence in the breaking of the bread. At the sending time, music is crucial. An uplifting, lively song serves as a "blast-off" to send teens forth.

What kind of music accomplishes these good things in a teen liturgy? First, the music must be relevant to teens. Relevant music does not equate to the latest best-selling hit. Usually this type of song is popular one day, not so the next. Rather, being "relevant" means taking good quality music that is appropriate for any liturgy and adapting it for use with teens. This is accomplished in several ways, but primarily through the use of instrumentation that is attractive to teens, like drums, electric bass, keyboard, and the electric guitar. The electric guitar is a symbol of the teen culture. It should be used in liturgy! Usually the appeal of a song for a teen has more to do with the arrangement of the song than the lyrics.

Besides instrumentation, the music must be exciting and life-filled. That's hard to describe precisely, except to say that it can't be stoic or boring. Teens want something with energy in it! They want to hear a song that is performed with joy, sincerity, and with them in mind. Music at liturgy can and should be reverent and prayerful, but this must be accomplished without sacrificing passion and appeal. Remember, effective music that reaches teens does not always have to be fast and loud; rather it should work well within the flow of the liturgy and fit well within each part of the Mass.

The music must have a sense of prayer. Participation is the goal to keep in mind. If the music is of professional quality, but the assembly is sitting with arms folded and not singing, then something is missing. A litmus test for determining whether the music at liturgy is hitting the mark is whether or not the congregation is "engaged." If the teens and the rest of the assembly are not singing and praying the music, then the goals of liturgical music are not being met.

The kind of music chosen for liturgy should, generally speaking, be singable, scriptural, and simple. Most of the music used should be liturgical and taken from liturgical music publishers like Oregon Catholic Press, GIA, World Library and Resource Publications.

Also, songs from contemporary Christian music artists like Kathy Troccoli, Amy Grant, Rich Mullins, Twila Paris, and others may be used.

What makes good music? A well-written piece of music will most always include quality, rhythm, melody, and harmony. Don't forget that with proper instrumentation and arrangement, almost any well-written and liturgically appropriate song can be effective with teens at Mass.

Finally, keep abreast of how the teens respond to the music. Watch the faces of the teens during the liturgy. Are they singing the songs that are chosen? Are they enthusiastic about the music? Knowing and responding to the needs of your assembly is the best indicator for doing effective music at teen liturgies.

Reflections on Music and Music Ministry

Live a Catholic Life *"Our song" is only as believable as our life. We must live our faith every day if we are to be leaders and ministers. When we have passion for Christ, the Church, and the sacraments, it will show in the performance of our ministry. When we lack the "fire of God," it is quite evident. You can't lead if you don't follow!*

Quality! *Three well-prepared musicians are always better than eight or ten well-meaning yet musically questionable "ministers." Start small and strong, and build from there.*

Choose Good Music *Songs that "worked" a couple of years ago may not be successful now. Choose music that is singable and well known, but intersperse some new music too! Don't choose what **you** want, but what **works!***

The "Key" Is the Key! *Just because the sheet music is written in G major doesn't mean you have to do it in that key. Lower it, raise it, or do whatever it takes to insure your assembly can sing it.*

Variety Is the Spice of Life *Try different musical styles and different instruments. Reggae, choral, praise, bluegrass, rock, pop, chant and so on. Percussion and vocals alone. Piano, synthesizer, strings, and a soloist. People love variety.*

Practice Makes Perfect! *Rehearsal is not optional. We owe it to the people of God. Spend the time working out arrangements, harmonies, and tempos. A true professional is the one who comes prepared.*

Tune Your Instrument/Tune Your Heart! *Part of being prepared is making sure we do some very basic things. Tune that guitar, and tune that flute. Make sure the piano is tuned every month or two and . . . "tune" your heart! Make sure you pray as a group before Mass and focus on what your role is. We musicians are called to be servants of the people of God.*

Get out of the Way! *Once we have picked solid music (and solid musicians), chosen the appropriate key, tuned our instruments and ourselves . . . then get out of the way. Encourage the assembly to sing in such a way that you are "drowned out" by their singing. When this happens you have done your job well.*

Go With the Flow *The liturgy has a powerful "ebb and flow." The presider most influences this flow, both positively and negatively. Work as a team. A good presider can sense the need for more reverence, more "spiritedness" or whatever. Listen and watch! You are providing the "music score" for a holy, ancient, and relevant rite.*

—Tom Booth
National Director of Music, LIFE TEEN
Mesa, Arizona

The Role of the Musician

First and foremost, the musicians at liturgy are ministers. Not only they, but those responsible for set-up and tear-down of the musical equipment, the mixing of sound, and any other much-needed work of this kind are involved in important ministries as well. That means that they should all think of themselves as ministers.

The musicians are there to serve the assembly. Musicians are "foot-washers." Their role is to help the people of God to pray and to sing. They are not there for their own glory, or to show people how good they are at music. Musicians must be rooted in their roles of service, as ministers of the gospel.

Part of the musician's responsibility is to keep an "ear to the pavement" of the present teen culture, never ignoring what teens are listening to on car radios or watching on television music channels like MTV. In a way, popular music is a window to the soul of today's teenagers. However, a music minister must keep in mind that his or her ministry is not validated by imitation of the teen music culture. Rather, music ministers must remain deeply rooted in Christ and not be threatened by what is happening on pop radio. By showing interest in the kind of music that teens listen to, music ministers are telling teens that they love and care about them enough to know what is important in their lives.

Music ministers should pursue excellence in humility and love. Music ministers also need to be creative and take chances. It is important, however, that they stay rooted in the faith and be mindful of what they are doing and why they are doing it. Use a variety of musical styles and keep the music alive. Remember: the bottom line is that teens are hungry for love, truth, and a sense of belonging, not the latest fad tune. Don't be afraid to turn down the volume, raise your hands, and lead your teens in heartfelt worship of the Creator. Serve them with your instruments and voices, for music is holy, good, and the most powerful tool we have in youth ministry today!

Excuse Me, Father, But We Need to Buy Some Drums

I can't tell you how many times visitors have come up to me after Mass and asked about the music. "We have no idea where to begin," they say. I want to sit down and talk with them for an hour, but usually don't have that much time. Instead, I simply say, "Do good music!"

What does that mean? It seems that a lot of people expect that we have to suddenly put on a show for teens. Nothing could be further from the truth. There are no fancy light tricks, no smoke machines, no large speaker stacks on either sides. We do not want anything that distracts from what's important: the proclamation and breaking open of God's Word and the breaking and sharing of Christ's body and blood.

Our job as musicians is to enhance the liturgy with good music. Good music is music that is well thought out, well played, and facilitates prayer and worship. Hence, my direction: "Do good music."

What else is good music? For starters, good music is music that is appropriate for Mass. Just because someone writes a song and calls it liturgical does not make it appropriate. For each song, I ask myself:

"Does this song facilitate prayer or is it just a cool song? Are people praising and praying with this song, or just dancing to it?" If the answers are the latter, then these songs are not for liturgy. As a general rule, after you do find a song that is appropriate for liturgy, look for ways to arrange it a little differently so that it speaks to the other things teens like in their music.

Good music is also music that is played well. Once you've chosen songs you want to use at Mass, practice them! Teens are definitely choosy about what they like and what they don't like. If they hear a group that is out of tune or can't stay together, or can't sing, they are not going to like it much. We are trying to draw teens in, not push them away. I think that being prepared is one of the most important lessons that I've learned in ministry. Look up from your music. Make eye contact with the congregation. Smile. Invite everyone to sing with you. You are not singing for them. You are simply leading them in song. That is why it is important to know your music well. If you don't know it, how can you lead?

Another common question is "What kind of instruments do we need in order to get started?" I always answer: "The basics." That means you need a set of drums, a bass guitar, a piano (or keyboard), and an acoustic guitar or two. You also need three to five singers. The response often comes back: "We have all those instruments. We have singers. It's just that no one is that good at them."

This is probably the biggest problem I've witnessed. There are many people who would love to offer their services, but not everyone is capable of doing so. In most cases, if you can find at least one or two other people who are strong musically, preferably someone who plays guitar or piano, they can act as leaders for both the congregation and the band. They can usually help to find other strong musicians as well. Look for those one or two people to form the core of the group, then go from there.

My after-Mass visitors also tell me that they "don't have the money to buy new equipment." This response is easy for me because neither did we. In fact, all the people who played in the band brought their own instruments. Some even brought speakers and microphones. Our equipment wasn't necessarily the best out there, but it worked until we got more financial support from people who liked what we were doing—ministering to the teens.

We practiced long and hard. When it finally came time for the first LIFE TEEN Mass, we were prepared and the liturgy was successful. If I could do those beginning Masses all over again, I would turn down the volume, soften up the drums, and be careful not to start or stop songs too abruptly. We learned as we went on. The band grew and the congregation grew right along with us.

All in all, music is a powerful thing. It can be inspiring or it can be distracting. Be careful and plan your music well. Pray your music well too.

—Edward A. Bolduc
Director of Music
St. Ann's Parish
Marietta, Georgia

Music in Other Settings

Good music also enhances many other elements of effective teen programming. Simply having a CD playing as teens walk into a meeting room can set a nice tone for what is to follow. Fun warm-up songs are a great way to grab a group's attention and get them interested in what is going on.

Soft, instrumental music for prayer or meditations during the meeting time also work well. Ending a meeting with a prayerful song—either reflective or uplifting—is a great way to send teens away from the meeting with the reminder to carry the message of the liturgy and the meeting to those who were not in attendance.

Part II

The LIFE TEEN Program

What Is LIFE TEEN?

LIFE TEEN in Brief

In April of 1985, when most teens were looking forward to the end of school and daydreaming of summer fun, there was one group of Arizona teens who had other plans. These teens gathered on a Sunday night for something called "LIFE TEEN," beginning with a Mass planned especially for them. After Mass, about 150 teens stayed to talk some more about Jesus and how he could change their lives.

This memorable night captured the attention of many more teens in the weeks that followed. Word spread about this new total youth ministry program to friends and families at nearby parishes. Now, over a decade later, the dream and vision of the LIFE TEEN program has reached thousands of teens in parishes across the United States and Canada.

Now, as it was in the beginning, LIFE TEEN is a parish-based program for high-school teens of all faiths. The goal of LIFE TEEN is to create an environment to lead teens into relationship with Jesus Christ and his Church. LIFE TEEN reaches teens on all levels: emotional, intellectual, spiritual, and social.

The LIFE TEEN program is centered on the Sunday Eucharist. It begins with a teen Mass followed immediately by a youth-only LIFE Night where issues are raised and teachings are covered, but primarily teens are led to a deeper relationship with Christ and challenged to live out the responsibilities of their faith journeys. Pouring out from the teen Mass, this is done in an atmosphere where teens feel loved and accepted both by their peers and adult leaders from the community who are there to serve them.

As with any youth ministry program, in order for LIFE TEEN to achieve its full potential, full support of the entire parish community is necessary. Particularly, the commitment of at least one priest to the program is essential. A priest is needed to preside at the weekly LIFE TEEN Mass and to facilitate prayer and do occasional teachings on Church doctrine at the LIFE Nights. Also, a youth minister is needed to work closely with the priest. The youth minister should have a good rapport with teens, be a person of faith, and have a good working knowledge of the Church. After an orientation and training in the LIFE TEEN program, the youth minister initiates, organizes, and oversees the program among a core group of adult leaders, parish leadership, and the parish at large.

The LIFE TEEN core group is comprised of adults who are at least out of high school and who are *not* a parent of a high-school teenager. The main job of a core member is to reach out to teens, both on an individual basis and a group basis. Also, the core members help with all LIFE Nights and retreats. A diverse core group of adults of different experiences, ages, genders, and the like helps to bring a great deal of creativity to the program.

Music is another fundamental component of the LIFE TEEN program. Music is a dominant force in the life of most teens. LIFE TEEN builds on this and uses music to nourish and foster the teens' faith and to center the teens' life in Christ. The use of effective, appropriate, and appealing music is most important in liturgy. For these reasons, the LIFE TEEN program requires a music minister who is both sensitive to teen interests and who is able to lead the assembly in powerful and prayerful melody.

The recipients of the labors of this ministry are the teenagers. LIFE TEEN provides the opportunity for teens to feel welcome and important in the Church. It provides the opportunity for teens to experience the connection between the Church and their everyday lives. Through a Mass geared especially for teens, the LIFE TEEN program presents an option for competing with the destructive, untruthful segments in our society. By taking part in LIFE TEEN on a weekly basis, teens are given the opportunity to serve others, and begin to do so with a willing spirit of joy. Through the LIFE TEEN experience, hearts are transformed and lives are forever changed.

As one teen said, "Through LIFE TEEN I am proud to be called a Catholic and do not hesitate to share the gracious love of our Savior with others. Keeping the Lord alive through prayer and great music is an awesome way to teach us about the holy Eucharist and the great sacrifice the Lord made for us."

LIFE TEEN Particulars

LIFE TEEN follows the Church's mandate to make Jesus Christ the center of everything we do. It is centered on Jesus, in particular Jesus in the Eucharist. To that end, LIFE TEEN is a total youth ministry program that tries to reach teens of all kinds. This means teens who are popular and those who are not, teens who are the best athletes and those who have never touched a ball. It is for teens of any economic status. LIFE TEEN is for teens of every race and cultural background.

LIFE TEEN is open to *all* high school teens in grades nine through twelve. It is important, however, not to include junior high teens in the LIFE TEEN program. Doing so labels it a "junior high" program and hinders older teens from coming. However, teens of all faiths are invited to come. LIFE TEEN offers a great opportunity for evangelization. LIFE TEEN has provided the impetus for many converts to Catholicism.

The goal of LIFE TEEN is to create an environment for teens to have their hearts transformed through encountering Jesus Christ. When this happens, teens are eager to learn more about their faith and evangelize and serve others.

LIFE TEEN Structure

LIFE TEEN meets throughout the year. A LIFE TEEN Mass followed by a LIFE Night meeting is held every Sunday. Occasionally, there is a Sunday without a LIFE Night meeting due to a holiday or scheduled LIFE TEEN trip, but the LIFE TEEN Mass is celebrated every Sunday of the year.

For purposes of establishing programming themes, the year is divided into three semesters: spring, summer, and fall.

Within this structure, no attendance is taken. There is no registration and no fees are collected. The reason for this is more easily to effect LIFE TEEN's goal of having teens come to a deep and personal relationship with Jesus. Teens cannot be coerced to such a relationship. In the same way, they only come to LIFE TEEN because they want to come, not because they have to come.

LIFE TEEN Components

As a Eucharist-centered program, the weekly LIFE TEEN Mass is the main component of the program. All other programming flows from the Mass and the encounter teens have with Jesus in the liturgy.

Admittedly, there are several factors that could prohibit a parish from committing to a weekly teen Mass. Some parishes may not have a priest who is in residence. In these cases, it may be wise to combine programming efforts with a neighboring parish. It is very difficult to conduct a successful LIFE TEEN program without a weekly teen liturgy.

The main component of LIFE TEEN outside the weekly Mass is the Sunday LIFE Nights. These are meetings that take place immediately after Mass. LIFE Nights run on four-week cycles within each semester. Two of the LIFE Nights in the cycle focus on educational topics like scripture, Christology, or sacraments. One of the LIFE Nights is called an "issue night" and covers hot-button topics like sexuality, suicide, or drug abuse. The fourth LIFE Night is a social night and is meant to give teens the opportunity to build new friendships. The purpose of the LIFE Night is to extend the community that has begun to form among the teens at Mass as well as to begin to explore in a deeper way some of the issues affecting them and the Church.

The Sunday LIFE TEEN Mass and LIFE Night encourage a deeper participation among the teens that must be facilitated with activities held throughout the week. Ongoing weekday components of the LIFE TEEN program may include a teen prayer group, a rap session, a Bible study or faith series, or a weekday lunch-time prayer (held at the church or the local high school). A LIFE House, or youth room, can be opened for scheduled drop-in hours throughout the week. In conjunction with the teen programming, a parent support group or parent education classes may also meet. Sometimes the parent support group meets at another place at the same time the teens are at a LIFE Night.

If the sacrament of confirmation is administered to high-school age students, a preparation program for teens can be held simultaneously in accordance with diocesan policies. Similarly, a Christian initiation process designed to include teens should also be in place to respond to teens who desire reception of Baptism and Eucharist.

Weekend retreats are held at least twice a year and a week-long leadership/discipleship camp is held every summer. These are opportunities for the teens to leave familiar surroundings and to devote special energy to developing a better relationship with themselves, others, and especially with Jesus Christ. Many different service projects including meal service to the poor, visiting the elderly, and collecting food and clothing for the homeless are ongoing. Also, LIFE TEEN offers several social trips throughout the year to the beach, theme parks, skiing resorts, and the like. Most of these social outings include the celebration of an outdoor Mass. More often than not, teens say that the Mass is the part of the trip that impacted them the most.

A History of LIFE TEEN

It all started in a small cafe off Route 66 . . . okay, not really, but it sounded interesting.

1977 *As a seminarian, Father Dale teaches a religious education class ("that I was terrible at"). A few months later, Fr. Dale finds that the top student in the class has left the Church. Says Fr. Dale: "When I asked him why, he said because he didn't feel loved in the Catholic Church. So I made the determination at that point that I was going to do everything I could to make sure our young people felt loved."*

1985 *Fr. Dale, youth minister Phil Baniewicz, and music minister Tom Booth begin youth program at St. Timothy's Catholic Church in Mesa, Arizona.*

Father Dale and Phil come up with name LIFE TEEN (over Chinese food—honestly), giving a strong indication that the program would not only stand up for the dignity of life, but that it would be life-giving for every teenager who became a part of it.

About 600 teens attend first LIFE TEEN Mass. Close to 200 of them remain for the first LIFE Night.

Within two months, the LIFE TEEN Mass averages over 1,000 teens, the LIFE Nights about 300 teens.

LIFE TEEN's first music group assembled. Some of the original members remain with the band today.

1987 *In January, Fr. Dale, Phil, and Tom began taping a television program for EWTN with topics such as peer pressure, searching for the truth, alcoholism, and sexuality. Fr. Jack Spaulding, pastor at St. Maria Goretti Church in Scottsdale, Arizona, joins the television team as a co-host.*

In conjunction with the television programming, a non-profit company, Catholic Life Productions (the forerunner of Catholic Life, Incorporated) is founded. The company's mission was to provide television programming on the Catholic faith, especially directed toward teenagers.

The first-ever television documentary on Medjugorje is produced by LIFE TEEN and aired in June on EWTN.

1988 *Due in great part to the nationwide broadcast of the television programs, St. Timothy's receives dozens of inquiries about its youth program. In the spring, with the help of core members from St. Tim's LIFE TEEN, a LIFE TEEN program is established at Our Lady of Mount Carmel in Tempe. Another program at St. Dorothy's in Glendora, California, is up and running a few months later. Both programs begin slowly, but grow rapidly.*

A few other Arizona parishes begin LIFE TEEN in the fall, including Fr. Jack Spaulding's parish.

To assist parishes in starting LIFE TEEN, a training package with three video tapes is produced.

Some LIFE TEEN staff members begin presenting workshops on youth ministry nationwide.

1989 *A LIFE TEEN slogan is established: "100% Catholic."*

1991 *The first national conference to assist parishes in orientation and training is held at St. Timothy's in the summer. (By 1996 these conferences are being held in hub parishes in different regions throughout the country.)*

1992 *Ann Virdagamo, a youth minister from New Orleans, organizes a three-day conference, giving teens the opportunity to experience LIFE TEEN first-hand.*

A national survey of LIFE TEEN parishes is conducted.

*The survey reveals the need for a subscription service. The service is started, including weekly liturgical planning guides, a toll-free hotline, training videos, a subscription to **You!** magazine, a discount on training conferences, and networking with other parishes who are involved with LIFE TEEN. One hundred parishes subscribe in the first year. (By the end of 1997, over 400 parishes come on board.)*

Television programming comes to an end. The focus of LIFE TEEN is turned exclusively toward parish-based ministry.

1993 *In February, well-known Christian music artist Kathy Troccoli performs a concert at St. Timothy's. Soon after, she agrees to be the first national spokesperson for LIFE TEEN.*

The National LIFE TEEN Event at World Youth Day in Denver is staged. The event includes music, video presentations, speakers, sharing, and a powerful eucharistic devotion during a two-hour period. Over 6,000 teens attend, with thousands more being turned away.

During a concert at World Youth Day, Kathy Troccoli announces her National Spokesperson title to a crowd of over 200,000.

After World Youth Day, hundreds of inquiries about LIFE TEEN come from all over North America.

1994 *In an effort to ensure quality control, the LIFE TEEN name is trademarked: ®!*

1995 *Regional hub parishes are designated in the Atlanta and Cleveland areas. St. Ann's Church in Marietta, Georgia, is the southeast hub. St. Mary's Church in Hudson, Ohio, is the northeast hub. Randy Raus and Beth Davis are named regional coordinators for the two areas.*

*A partnership with Veritas Communications, publishers of **You!** magazine is formed. Paul Lauer, editor of **You!**, creates a LIFE TEEN page in every issue of the magazine.*

LIFE TEEN is presented to Pope John Paul II. Fr. Dale, Randy Raus, and Kathy Troccoli take a group of 100 teens on a pilgrimage to Assisi and Rome. They are presented to Pope John Paul II at a weekly audience. The Holy Father gives his blessing to the LIFE TEEN program.

1996 *Nationally-known chastity educator Mary Beth Bonacci is hired as a special LIFE TEEN consultant. She creates a LIFE Night resource for youth ministers to aid them in presenting the topics of sexuality and chastity.*

To further the ability to reach teens through the media, a 4,000-square-foot media center and television studio is completed in Phoenix. The capital campaign is aided by former Arizona governor Rose Mofford, NBA star Kevin Johnson, and famed pizza maker Rose Totino.

Opening in June, the studio is given the name Life Studios. Television programming, audio recordings, videos and other multi-media projects are planned.

*A new training package is completed, including three videos. Rachel Campos, a former LIFE TEEN member and past cast member on MTV's **Real World**, hosts the videos.*

Plans are under way for a LIFE TEEN Camp in Yarnell, Arizona. Nearly 150 acres are purchased to turn this dream into a reality. The camp will host LIFE TEEN programs and retreats and sponsor several summer camping opportunities.

LIFE TEEN also pursues a site in Atlanta for a second camp.

1997 *LIFE TEEN joins with Franciscan University of Steubenville to host a youth conference in Cave Creek, Arizona. Over 1,000 teens attend.*

1998 *This book you are reading is published.*

Getting Started/Leadership Roles

Starting a LIFE TEEN Program

If you've ever experienced a LIFE TEEN Mass, you no doubt witnessed hundreds of teenagers with arms reverently linked gathered around the altar. Likely, you also heard a priest who addressed teen issues and music that was appealing for prayer and praise. After Mass, many teens remained for more fellowship, dialogue, study, and prayer. If you were there, you participated in a situation that propelled your spirit and that of the entire worshipping community.

Being a spokesperson for LIFE TEEN has been an honor and a blessing for me. I believe that LIFE TEEN is making a huge impact on the youth of America. Seeing these kids truly come to know God in ways they have not, and seeing them worship with all their hearts has been so exciting! The meetings have been a haven for them to share their fears, failures, struggles, and dreams in a time when there is extreme pressure on them to be tossed by the wind of lies. LIFE TEEN brings them the absolute truth of the gospel and the standards of Christ. It's more than just learning about rules: they are truly learning to live for him and know that God wants the very best for them.

—Kathy Troccoli
LIFE TEEN National Spokesperson

The question is: how can any parish get to the same point in its ministry with youth? The first step is to work collaboratively among several different people and groups in the parish. The support of each of the following is crucial to the success of the program:

Pastor

The pastor must be committed to doing a weekly teen Mass and to leading prayer at the end of the LIFE Night. He should also be willing to do an occasional teaching on Church doctrine at the LIFE Nights. If the pastor is unable to make these commitments, an associate pastor can be assigned to do so. However, it is important that the pastor is informed of the overall scope of the LIFE TEEN program so that he can offer his support by helping to announce the program to the parish, by approving of related expenses (snacks, reproducible handouts, musician stipends, youth minister's salary, and so on). If money truly is not available for LIFE TEEN, the pastor must allow for the opportunity for fundraising to begin the program and for keeping it vital.

Parish Leadership

The LIFE TEEN program should be presented to various parish groups like the parish council, finance committee, or education committee. (It is strongly recommended that these groups are shown the first fifteen minutes of LIFE TEEN Training Video 1, "Overview of the Teen Culture and LIFE TEEN," Catholic Life, Incorporated.)

In addition, other parish groups like the Young Adult Ministry, Women's Fellowship, Men's Spirituality, or related organizations like the Knights of Columbus should be made aware of the plans for implementing LIFE TEEN. These groups can then be counted on to help promote the program with publicity, and in some cases financially.

Youth Minister

A youth minister should be in place at the parish for the start of LIFE TEEN programming. It is important that a youth minister be a person who (1) loves the faith, (2) will take charge of the program, and (3) can reach teenagers. It is also helpful if the youth minister is organized and creative. One of the main responsibilities of the youth minister will be to oversee the core group and allow its members to also reach out to teens. It is recommended that the youth minister be given a salary or at least a stipend. If this is not possible, it is still necessary for one person to be designated as youth minister to take responsibility for the overseeing of the program.

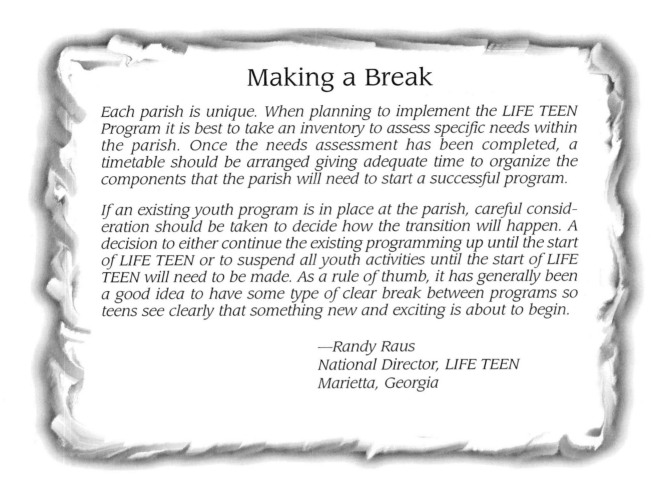

Making a Break

Each parish is unique. When planning to implement the LIFE TEEN Program it is best to take an inventory to assess specific needs within the parish. Once the needs assessment has been completed, a timetable should be arranged giving adequate time to organize the components that the parish will need to start a successful program.

If an existing youth program is in place at the parish, careful consideration should be taken to decide how the transition will happen. A decision to either continue the existing programming up until the start of LIFE TEEN or to suspend all youth activities until the start of LIFE TEEN will need to be made. As a rule of thumb, it has generally been a good idea to have some type of clear break between programs so teens see clearly that something new and exciting is about to begin.

—Randy Raus
National Director, LIFE TEEN
Marietta, Georgia

Core Group

The core group is essential to having a good LIFE TEEN program. The core team are people, like the youth minister, who are charged with reaching out to teens. Therefore, core members must be able to relate well to teens. They shouldn't be people who communicate a "know-it-all" attitude to teens. Rather, they should be compassionate people who are able to share their personal experiences but also are able to listen well to the experiences of the teens.

Core members should be a diverse group with lots of different talents and interests. Some core members may be outgoing and able to share a story or teaching at the drop of a hat. Other core members may be more reserved, yet better able to reach out to the shy or lonely teen. Core members can be found by approaching prospective candidates after Sunday Masses, in parish young adult groups, or at a neighboring college through a Newman Center.

Also, as teens graduate from the LIFE TEEN program, they often make excellent core members. There should be at least 15 to 20 core members; upwards of 30 members is even better.

The only people who should *not* be core members are parents of teenagers and high school students. LIFE Nights are marked by deep sharing. Teens feel a reluctance to share when their parents or the parents of their peers are around. Likewise, other high school students should not be a part of the group.

Music Minister

A music minister is essential to having quality music at a LIFE TEEN Mass. The music minister should have some familiarity with the teen culture and teen music and be able to adapt liturgical songs through proper instrumentation to appeal to teens. The music minister should at least be paid a stipend.

Musicians may be found in many places, including college music programs (and the Newman Center). When the music minister has talent and energy, he or she will be able to attract and assemble a quality band. It is better to start with a smaller group of quality people and to allow the group to evolve slowly than with a larger group whose purpose is mainly to provide the widest assembly of instrumentation and choir.

It's essential that the music minister and the band and choir be trained in liturgy so that they will have a clear understanding of how good music is able to enhance it.

Before beginning the program, a meeting with the parents should be held to let them know what the program is about. The parents should be given an overview of the program in as much detail as possible (LIFE TEEN Training Video 1 works well for this.) and asked to support the program through encouraging their children to attend and by helping them to do so. After the program is up and running, a parent support group may be formed. This is a group that can meet on Sundays to discuss parenting issues and other issues relevant to the lives of teens while the teens are at LIFE Night.

Top Ten Songs of the LIFE TEEN Program

1. *Awesome God* Rich Mullins, BMG Music, Inc. (Gospel Division)

2. *Go Light Your World* Chris Rice, BMG Music, Inc. (Gospel Division)

3. *He Is Exalted* Twila Paris, Straightway Music

4. *Holy Is His Name* Jon Michael Talbot, Birdwing Music

5. *I Will Choose Christ* Tom Booth and Kathy Troccoli, De Cristo Music/Sony Tree Publishing Co. (BMI)

6. *Make Us A Eucharistic People* Julie and Tim Smith, Resource Publications

7. *My Life Is In Your Hands* Kathy Troccoli and Bill Montvilo, Emily Booth Inc. (adm. by Reunion Music)/Floating Note Music, Inc.

8. *Profession of Faith* Tom Booth, Oregon Catholic Press

9. *Rain Down* Ed Bolduc, World Library Publications

10. *We Are One Body* R. Scallon, Heartbeat Music

No More Objections

My oldest son began participating in the LIFE TEEN Program at St. Thérèse Church of the Little Flower when he was a freshman in high school. My second son is now participating. The LIFE TEEN Program has been an answer from God for me and my sons. It had not been easy to bring the boys to Mass every Sunday with objections such as "It is boring. Why do I have to go?" Since we started to go to the LIFE TEEN Mass, I don't hear those objections any longer.

The LIFE TEEN liturgy has made a big difference in our lives. The music, singing, and liturgical movements have all contributed in making Mass a praising, glorious celebration. With the older son singing and playing the congas, he has a certain ownership in the liturgy which has helped in his spiritual growth. His faith has also grown by his participating in other activities with the LIFE TEEN group. He goes on retreats and he is involved in a prayer group. If there is an activity (helping the Knights of Columbus or other group, fundraising, etc.) he is willingly involved. He has made close friends. Even more importantly, he is closer to God.

The LIFE TEEN program has made our—my sons' and my own—faith more tangible and generous. Now that we know how blessed we are to have this gift of faith, we are more willing to enthusiastically share it with others.

—Lorna J. Hornbuckle
St. Thérèse Church of the Little Flower
Reno, Nevada

Teens

The LIFE TEEN program is for teens. Laying the groundwork for the program means inviting teens to participate. This means talking with teens after Mass and going to places where teens are. The first group of teens that should be targeted are teens who are leaders among their peer groups. For example, it is wise to make note of Catholic teens who are captains of their athletic teams, honor students, student officers, and the like and to then approach them with the charge to get involved. When other teens see these so-called "cool" people participating, they will understand that LIFE TEEN is for everyone.

Also, the teens should always be reminded to invite their friends to LIFE TEEN. Remember, LIFE TEEN is for all high school students, Catholics and non-Catholics. It is up to the involved teens to reach out to the uninvolved teens.

Finally, consider doing a publicity blitz among the teens prior to the start-up of the program. Hand out flyers, LIFE TEEN T-shirts and hats, and any other publicity aids that will help to get the word out.

Step by Step

With great fear and reservation as to what I was going to find, I proceeded to go to my first LIFE TEEN Mass and LIFE Night. Though the group of teens in attendance was small in size, it was as if a flame blazed within each individual heart present, letting off a warmth that chased away the chill of that cold, rainy April night. I would have never thought that exactly a year later, to the day, I would be baptized and confirmed in the Catholic Church.

Through the duration of that year I grew in so many ways. First, taking small steps much like that of a child, the once dull and cold embers that resided within my heart began to glow. It was there in the youth group that I had finally found the treasure that I had searched for—the warmth that I had tried so desperately to find.

Many teens see the inspiration in their lives to be a movie star or a prominent sports figure, but to me, it cannot go without saying that my youth ministers were the inspiration in my life—they were the light that set my heart on fire. It seemed only fitting that I chose them for my godparents.

—Leah Moser
St. John Catholic Church
Chico, California

Leadership Responsibilities

To have a successful LIFE TEEN program, the leaders need to know their roles. Once the priest, youth minister, music minister, and core team know what is expected of them and each other, each will minister more effectively than ever before. Here is some more detail on the responsibilities for each of these leaders.

Responsibilities of the Priest

A priest's ongoing presence among teens has a great and lasting impact. A dynamic style or personality may be helpful, but it is not necessary. A sincere and genuine willingness to be with teens is the only major qualification.

Since LIFE TEEN is a Eucharist-centered program, the first responsibility of the priest is to preside at Mass. Along with this role, he must be able to relate a homily to teens and he must be involved in the planning of the Mass.

The priest should also be a participant in the LIFE Nights. He should know the topics being addressed in the LIFE Nights, approving of the content and helping to make sure that the material distilled is in line with Church teaching. The priest doesn't have to attend the entire LIFE Night, but he should make himself available to lead the closing prayer. Occasionally, he should plan to be the primary LIFE Night facilitator or catechist.

Weekend retreats are an important part of LIFE TEEN. Again, the priest should be involved with its planning and approval of its content. When the teens go on retreat, they should expect to be able to celebrate Eucharist. The priest should plan to preside at an opening and/or closing Mass. Also, retreats are an excellent opportunity for teens to examine their consciences and to celebrate the sacrament of reconciliation. The priest may not need to be at the retreat the entire weekend (although this is the ideal). However, he should plan at least to lead both the sacraments of Eucharist and reconciliation.

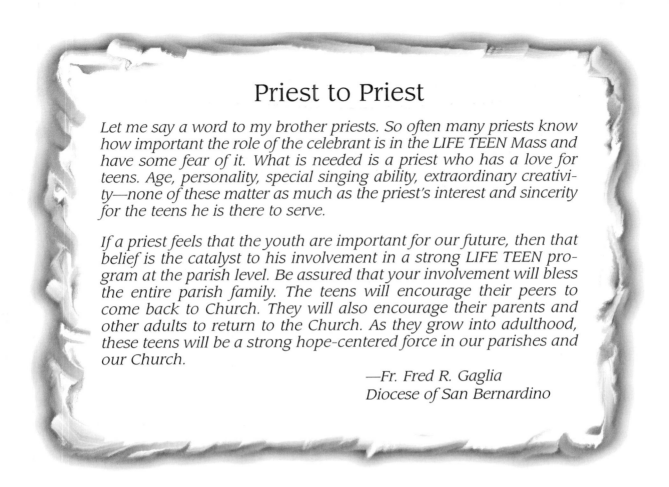

Priest to Priest

Let me say a word to my brother priests. So often many priests know how important the role of the celebrant is in the LIFE TEEN Mass and have some fear of it. What is needed is a priest who has a love for teens. Age, personality, special singing ability, extraordinary creativity—none of these matter as much as the priest's interest and sincerity for the teens he is there to serve.

If a priest feels that the youth are important for our future, then that belief is the catalyst to his involvement in a strong LIFE TEEN program at the parish level. Be assured that your involvement will bless the entire parish family. The teens will encourage their peers to come back to Church. They will also encourage their parents and other adults to return to the Church. As they grow into adulthood, these teens will be a strong hope-centered force in our parishes and our Church.

—Fr. Fred R. Gaglia
Diocese of San Bernardino

Responsibilities of the Youth Minister

The youth minister is both a minister to the teens and the minister to the core group. Overseeing all components of LIFE TEEN, the youth minister is the person who is in the background, making sure that everything runs like clockwork. The youth minister is heavily involved in both the planning of the LIFE TEEN Mass and the LIFE Night. The youth minister should be in weekly contact with the priest in regards to planning and implementation of these components.

Of course the primary tasks of the youth minister do not involve desk work. Rather, the youth minister must devote a great amount of time to getting out of the office and visiting the schools and other places where the teens are, making the effort to know them and talk with them on a one-to-one basis. Besides being able to relate well with teens, other qualifications for a youth minister include having a good working knowledge of the Church and Church doctrine, being trained in LIFE TEEN, living an appropriate Catholic Christian lifestyle, and having the desire and ability to help other people, namely the core group and teens.

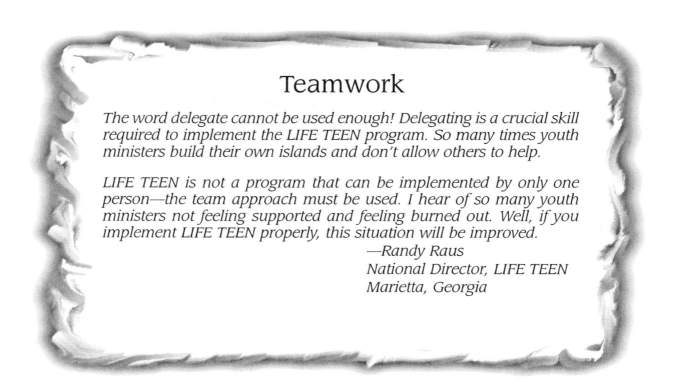

Teamwork

The word delegate cannot be used enough! Delegating is a crucial skill required to implement the LIFE TEEN program. So many times youth ministers build their own islands and don't allow others to help.

LIFE TEEN is not a program that can be implemented by only one person—the team approach must be used. I hear of so many youth ministers not feeling supported and feeling burned out. Well, if you implement LIFE TEEN properly, this situation will be improved.

—Randy Raus
National Director, LIFE TEEN
Marietta, Georgia

Responsibilities of the Music Minister

The music minister should first of all be a good musician who is able to lead others in song, either on the piano or guitar. He or she should live a life of faith and have a discernible love for God and the Church.

The music minister should be able to attract other good musicians who also meet the above qualifications. Usually the members of the band are not teenagers. Musicians need a level of spiritual and musical maturity. If a particular teen has that, then he or she may be used. Otherwise, the music should reach teens, though they should not lead it.

Also, the music minister should be actively involved in the planning of the liturgy and the selection of the songs. He or she will also schedule and lead rehearsals. Generally, one rehearsal takes place during the week, another before Sunday Mass.

Finally, the music minister or his designated replacement should be present at the LIFE Nights and on the retreats, primarily to lead prayer with song.

Responsibilities of Core Members

Being a core member means being at the heart of the LIFE TEEN program. Core membership requires approximately seven to ten hours of weekly commitment, including a Sunday night commitment of five hours for a meeting before Mass, Mass itself, LIFE Night, and clean-up. In addition, a core member can expect to spend some additional time during the week planning for LIFE Night sessions or a retreat, dropping by the youth center, and being present to teens at one of their activities (such as a high school football game).

Core members work under the leadership of the priest and the youth minister. Three to five core members take responsibility for planning and leading each LIFE Night. (See pages 51-52 for suggestions.) As their turn approaches, these core members should plan to turn in an outline of the LIFE Night to the youth minister at least two weeks before the LIFE Night will take place. This allows the youth minister time to review the plan and to help with any necessary adjustments.

All core members should plan to attend the LIFE TEEN Mass and LIFE Night each week, sitting among the teens and participating actively. Core members also plan and attend all retreats. In any situation, core members are expected to reach out to new teens, extending a warm invitation and encouraging them to come back again.

Finally, core members will likely be party to a great deal of sensitive information from the teens. They should recognize that they are not professional counselors and be willing to refer serious problems (such as bulimia, depression, drug abuse) to those competent to handle them. Also, core members must always represent official Church teaching and not their own personal opinions. When a teen asks a difficult question that a core member does not know, he or she must be willing to admit that but add, "I'll find out the answer for you."

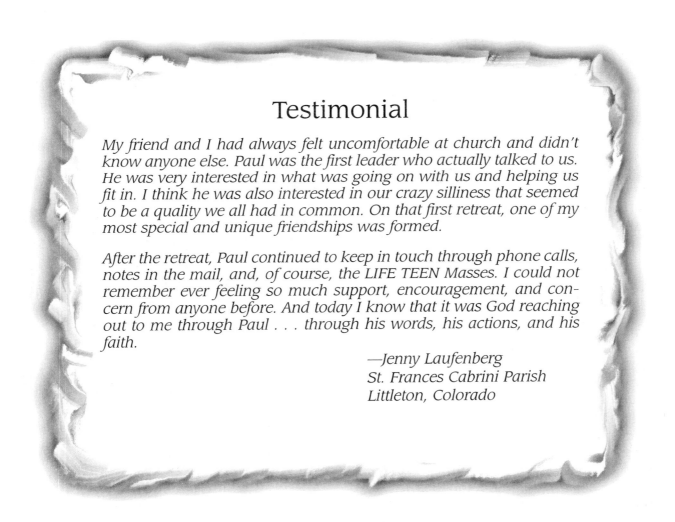

Testimonial

My friend and I had always felt uncomfortable at church and didn't know anyone else. Paul was the first leader who actually talked to us. He was very interested in what was going on with us and helping us fit in. I think he was also interested in our crazy silliness that seemed to be a quality we all had in common. On that first retreat, one of my most special and unique friendships was formed.

After the retreat, Paul continued to keep in touch through phone calls, notes in the mail, and, of course, the LIFE TEEN Masses. I could not remember ever feeling so much support, encouragement, and concern from anyone before. And today I know that it was God reaching out to me through Paul . . . through his words, his actions, and his faith.

—Jenny Laufenberg
St. Frances Cabrini Parish
Littleton, Colorado

Quality Teen Liturgy

A Look at the LIFE TEEN Mass

Celebrating a quality LIFE TEEN Mass takes efficient planning. This begins by taking the scriptures for the week and asking, "What are they saying?" and "What are they saying for us?" The "us" is always the teens.

Many priests and other adults involved in liturgy doubt that they can do a teen liturgy because of their distance from the teen experience. It is important that this issue be addressed: it is not enough for a homilist to be able to explain what the readings mean; in a LIFE TEEN Mass, he must also be able to connect the meaning of the readings with the teen's experience. If that experience is something the homilist and other liturgy planners are not in touch with, they should collaborate with people who do understand the lives of teenagers: youth ministers, core members, or teens themselves.

If a LIFE TEEN Mass were only done once every four or six weeks the planning, needless to say, would be much easier. Since a LIFE TEEN Mass is held every week, an effective system for ongoing planning and preparation must be in place. This includes holding regular training for lectors and music rehearsals. Special features, like skits or songs shared during homily time, demand more detailed preparation.

Having a meaningful Mass also involves paying close attention to the flow of the liturgy. One of the key elements is to make sure the musicians have a good sense of the flow (gather, proclaim, break, send). There are many built-in transitions in Mass. The musicians and the presider need a good working arrangement—and a strong sense of teamwork—so that the transitions between song and spoken parts are smooth.

The priest/presider has a central role as one who is animator of the celebration. He needs to be tuned in to the response of the assembly. Like the conductor of an orchestra, he must respond to the ebbs and flows through gestures of hospitality and warmth. Following his good lead, the rest of the assembly is charged with their calls to minister to one another.

The Mass is not a monologue, but a dialogue between priest and people. With their strong responses, the entire assembly becomes ministers of the Word, Eucharist, and hospitality. Listed below are some suggestions for enhancing and accommodating each of the main parts of the Mass so they appeal more to teens.

Gather

Entrance to the church. The word *ecclesia,* church, means "gathering." If you are going to have a human gathering, people are going to have relationships. To have relationships, means you have to talk. There is a lot of noise at the start of a LIFE TEEN Mass. It's the sound of teens renewing relationships with one another and welcoming those who are there for the first time. Some other teens may be handing out song sheets. And the priest may walk through the foyer or gathering space greeting and welcoming the assembly. It is absolutely essential to create a spirit of hospitality.

People Called to Their Seats. Right before the time of the Mass, the priest goes to the microphone and invites everyone inside. He may ask, "Does everyone have a song sheet?" This is an indicator that it's time to begin.

Music Rehearsal. Before the Mass begins, the music group takes its place and the music leader leads the rehearsal of every song that will be sung at Mass. This, too, is done in a friendly way. Besides warming up the singing voices of the assembly, it encourages the charge of Vatican II for full, active, and conscious participation at Mass. It's hard to have that if the assembly is not well-versed in the songs.

Official Greeting. The priest officially welcomes the assembly: authenticity and sincerity are the most important elements of the greeting. He introduces visitors from out of town. Then the assembly takes a few minutes to greet each other. While the greeting is taking place, the presider takes his place in the back of the church for the processional.

Opening Song. The whole purpose of the opening song is to bring people together as one and to heighten their participation. A long instrumental introduction is usually played as a sign that the liturgy is beginning and that the assembly should settle into an interior posture of prayer. It is important that the piece of music is easy to sing and is clearly related to the feast of the day or the "thrust" of the gospel reading. It should draw the assembly into the act of worship. The procession by the priests, deacon, lectors, cross bearer, and so on is also very important. They should not move too quickly. Each person in the procession should reverence the altar. The opening song should be continued instrumentally and quietly during the sign of the cross and can be reprised later (usually the refrain only) after the opening prayer.

Penitential Rite. The penitential rite is highlighted and sung during Lent at the LIFE TEEN Mass. Different treatments may be used in other Church seasons.

Gloria. The Gloria should be sung on appropriate feast days and seasons (Easter and Christmas, for example). It may be highlighted with sacred dance using banners and ribbons. Also allow the assembly to be expressive and sing out. The presider sets the tone by raising his hands and joining in the singing.

Opening Prayer. The priest says: "Will you please open your hands and pray with me?" Open hands are a sign of the resurrection of Christ. The early Church prayed in this same way. Some people are hesitant to express themselves in this way at first, but they soon embrace it through the example of the priest and the rest of the assembly. After the opening prayer, the priest asks the assembly to listen to, and be open to the proclamation of the readings. This is not only practically helpful to the gathered assembly, but also smoothes the transition from the "gather" to "proclaim."

Proclaim

The First and Second Readings. The first and second readings are done by teen lectors. It is essential that these teens have prepared well ahead of time. Training involves making sure the lectors (1) understand the importance of what they are doing; (2) have some knowledge about the background of the reading; (3) have a grasp of the meaning of the reading and what it should communicate; (4) use a clear and strong voice while proclaiming the Word of God. There are also other ways to proclaim a reading besides simply reading it. "Reader's Theatre" utilizes a narrator and two to three other readers who take the parts of "characters" in the reading. The use of slides with dimmed lighting and instrumental music is also effective when paired with a reading. If the reading is poetic and lends itself accordingly, it is sometimes effective to have a cantor sing the reading for special emphasis.

Psalm Response. Between the first and second readings is the responsorial psalm. There are a myriad of ways to present the psalm response. Choice of style (reflective, chant, light rock, gospel) is only one of the decisions to be made. Choice of musical form is another consideration: for example, call/response or refrain/verse. Also, a teen can proclaim the verses as the assembly responds by singing the refrain.

Sign language or simplified hand motions to express the psalm also work well. They should be practiced with the assembly before the Mass, however. Most importantly, the musical piece should be user-friendly. The key, tempo, and style should be simple and easy to sing. When accessible music is provided, the assembly will really want to sing and respond.

Gospel Acclamation. This is a time for really "getting into" a spirit of praise. Hands can be raised high. A gospel procession highlights this part of the liturgy. The book of gospels should be treated reverently and raised high as the priest or deacon processes to the ambo.

Gospel. While reading, the book of gospels should continue to be held high. Sometimes, other readers, accompanying slides, or the use of instrumental music played lightly "under" the gospel reading can be very powerful. In any case, the gospel should be well-proclaimed, with the priest or deacon looking up to the assembly during the reading for eye contact. At the end of the reading, the gospel alleluia or a reprise of the chorus of the opening song may be sung again.

Homily. This is a key part to the LIFE TEEN Mass. It must be addressed to the teens so that it draws them in. Creativity is key. Humor works well and skits can be a great way to involve young people. Calling teens forward and interviewing them with questions related to readings is also effective. Props (like actual milk and honey related to "the land of milk and honey") are also attention-getting. Finally, if possible, the priest should use a cordless microphone. This allows for freedom of movement.

Creed/Prayers of the Faithful. The priest should lead the creed and prayers of the faithful. A song setting of the creed can be a powerful way for the assembly to express their faith.

Break

Preparation of the Gifts. To reinforce teen ownership of the Mass, the teens bring the bread and wine forward, as well as take up the collection. Having the teens "set the table" is a powerful sign and simple task. Sometimes this can be done quite beautifully to the accompaniment of sacred dancers. After they set the table, the teens step back, reverence the altar, but remain in the sanctuary. Shortly after, all the teens will be invited around the altar. Those who set the table are the first to model this.

Eucharistic Prayer. Inviting the teens around the altar is of great importance at a LIFE TEEN Mass. This one simple gesture communicates volumes to the teens, above all, that the Lord is accessible, loving, intimate, and forgiving, and that the Church is the same. By inviting the teens to come up around the altar, the Church is saying to them: "We believe you are holy and that God is calling you to holiness," and "We believe the presence of Jesus is transforming and intimate and we want you to be close to it." Some teens may feel awkward coming around the altar. They should be encouraged to do so by core members and teen leaders. Since more and more new teens will always be coming to Mass, encouraging the teens to move to the front is an ongoing task. This practice is not intended to separate the community, but to allow the youth to minister to the community by giving witness to their faith and allowing the community, as a whole, to minister back to the teens. Remember, there should be no false barriers keeping anyone from Christ.

After the time the Holy, Holy is sung, all music should cease in order to highlight the eucharistic prayer and the reality of Christ's Real Presence. Silence is also a way to encourage reverence. The eucharistic acclamations provide an opportunity for the assembly to sing and respond, thus continuing the dialogue between priest and people.

Great Amen. The assembly's response to the eucharistic prayer is the Great Amen, signifying their agreement to all that has gone on before. The Great Amen should be sung with great vigor and passion; it may be a time when some of the teens raise their arms spontaneously as a sign of praise.

The Lord's Prayer. A simple arrangement of the Our Father is encouraged. Also, it is recommended that one arrangement be used consistently so that the teens can become familiar with it and "own it." Prior to the Our Father, the presider asks everyone to join together to display and encourage unity.

Sign of Peace. Certainly the energy and noise level goes up at a LIFE TEEN Mass during the Sign of Peace. The sign expressed should communicate warmth and affection. The Sign of Peace isn't a time to say "hello" to one another. Rather, it is a time to recognize the presence of Christ in the people who are there. If the noise level or behavior does become inappropriate, it is important for the core members sprinkled through the assembly to remind the teens of this. Music helps to keep this time reverent and not overly filled with commotion; the end of the music also helps to communicate closure to this time.

Lamb of God. The Lamb of God calls the assembly to focus around the altar. It is important that it be sung.

Communion. Before communion, the presider makes two announcements. First, he reminds the assembly to be reverent as they receive the body and blood of Christ. Second, he invites teens who are not Catholic to come before the priest or deacon and ask for a blessing. The request for a blessing can be indicated by having the teens cross their arms. The teachings of the Church do not allow non-Catholics to receive the sacraments and this teaching should be followed. Core members are often eucharistic ministers.

During Communion. During communion, the kind of music that is played is important. The song should be a prayerful, simple, Eucharist-based, and fairly well-known. Remember, people do not carry a song sheet with them to communion.

After Communion. After communion is a time for thanksgiving. It is also a great time for prayer and praise. A second song calls the assembly to a time of meditation or a time of praise. It may be a song sung by a soloist. During the song, the celebrant can kneel before the altar, indicating that the assembly is to do the same. Or, the celebrant may stand, face the altar, and raise his arms in praise. The assembly will spontaneously join in.

Closing Prayer. The presider and assembly stand for the closing prayer.

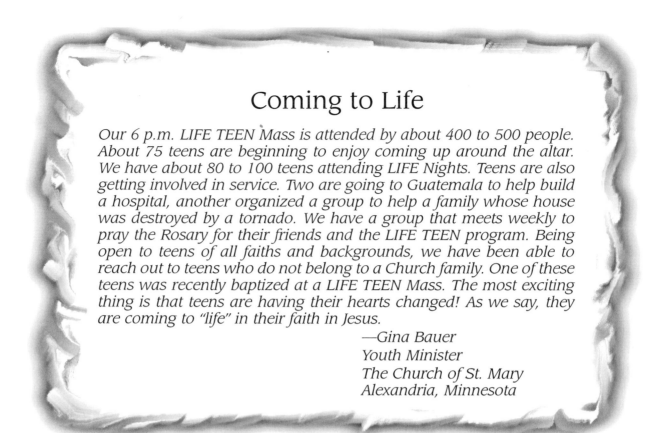

Coming to Life

Our 6 p.m. LIFE TEEN Mass is attended by about 400 to 500 people. About 75 teens are beginning to enjoy coming up around the altar. We have about 80 to 100 teens attending LIFE Nights. Teens are also getting involved in service. Two are going to Guatemala to help build a hospital, another organized a group to help a family whose house was destroyed by a tornado. We have a group that meets weekly to pray the Rosary for their friends and the LIFE TEEN program. Being open to teens of all faiths and backgrounds, we have been able to reach out to teens who do not belong to a Church family. One of these teens was recently baptized at a LIFE TEEN Mass. The most exciting thing is that teens are having their hearts changed! As we say, they are coming to "life" in their faith in Jesus.

—Gina Bauer
Youth Minister
The Church of St. Mary
Alexandria, Minnesota

Send

Announcements. The assembly sits for the announcements. First, the priest gives the general parish announcements that apply to the teens or their families. Next, the youth minister comes forward and dialogues with the priest in a lighthearted and creative way about the upcoming LIFE Night and any other teen events. The objectives are to let the teens know you love them and to encourage full participation of the teens who are there.

Final Blessing. The presider begins the final blessing with "The Mass . . . ." A LIFE TEEN tradition is for the assembly to jump in and say: " . . . never ends.

So let's go forth to love and serve the Lord. Thanks be to God. Alleluia." The reason for this format is to help the teens make the connection between living their lives and the celebration of the liturgy.

Closing Song. This is the time to go for it! Encourage clapping. The song should be upbeat, singable, and fun. The closing song sends the teens into the LIFE Night.

LIFE Nights

Gather the Teens After Mass

The LIFE Night is the follow-up gathering of teens after the LIFE TEEN Mass. During the announcements at the end of the Mass, the teens are told by the priest or youth minister the topic of LIFE Night and strongly encouraged to attend. Stimulating interest is important to getting the teens to stay for the LIFE Night. This can be done with short skits or impromptu music by the band during the announcement time.

LIFE Nights are held in an adjacent church room or hall. The room should not be so large that it seems empty when all the teens have gathered. It's better to use a smaller space and have the teens energized and bulging out the door. Setting up dividers in a larger room can help make the space more intimate. Core members gather at the entrance to invite teens in and greet those who are there for the first time.

Themes for Education Nights

Each theme may be the focus of one semester over the course of four years.

- Person of Jesus
- Introducing the Bible
- Relationships

- Witness/Service
- The Mass
- In-Depth Bible Study

- Sacraments
- Basic Moral Teaching
- Different Forms of Prayer/Mary

- Foundations of Faith/Catholic Identity
- Sexuality
- Life Choices Made With the Spirit

Hot Topics for Issue Nights

suicide	drugs
cults	occult
music	war and peace
dysfunctional families	dating
peer pressure	violence
future	materialism
love vs. infatuation	body language
communication with peers and parents	

---

sexual harassment	sex
rosary	Blessed Mother
honesty	pro-life
death and dying	addictions
eating disorders	humor
respect	media
sin	anger
divorce	

LIFE Night Planning

After the semester topics are scheduled and/or approved by the youth minister and priest, three to five core members are assigned to each LIFE Night. Those core members are responsible for carrying out the LIFE Night activities, including all of the planning steps before the LIFE Night even takes place.

The general cycle for LIFE Nights is to have two education nights, one issue night, and one social night every four weeks. Education nights are the main focus of the semester (for example, "the person of Jesus" or "basic moral teaching of the Church"). Issue nights cover topics especially relevant to teens, like relationships, vocations, leadership roles, or sexuality. The main focus of social nights is purely on fun and fellowship. These nights can be holiday dances, sporting events, or theme dinners. It is recommended that the first LIFE Night of a semester be a night of pizza and a rap session to remind teens that LIFE TEEN is not based in traditional classroom structure. No matter what is planned for, every LIFE Night ends in prayer with a Hail Mary followed by singing a simple rendition of the Ave Maria.

The first planning meeting of the core members is a brainstorming session in which the core determines their own—and the teens'—knowledge and expertise on the topic. They also establish a goal for the night—what they expect the teens to take away from the night—and then work backwards to determine ways to meet that goal.

The structure of the LIFE Night follows that of the LIFE TEEN Mass: Gather, Proclaim, Break, and Send.

The Gather portion of the night is meant to draw the teens in and welcome them; it can take the forms of a skit, video, or dramatic reading, serving not only to welcome the teens but to break the ice and set the mood for the rest of the evening. This is a great place to incorporate humor and interaction among the teens.

Proclaim is the time when the main message of the night is communicated to the teens. In a typical setting, this would involve a "teacher" telling information to "students." However, at a LIFE Night this portion must be done much more creatively. The brainstorming session usually uncovers many creative ways to get the main message across.

During the Break portion of the night, the message is distilled so that the teens can explore more deeply how it impacts their own lives. This usually involves having the teens meet in small groups and allowing for the opportunity for them to share personal responses to these issues. Preparing thoughtful questions or sentence-starters is vital to the success of the Break time.

Prayer is an important part of the Send portion of the session. Adoration, personal petitions shared by the teens, and even a closing song related to the night's topic work well. The important thing to remember is that the teens should be sent out with the positive charge and impetus to change their lives and the lives of others.

Once the core members establish what will take place in each segment of the LIFE Night, an overall timing schedule for the evening is created. The entire plan is written up and shared with the youth minister and priest. (Sample planning sheets are provided on pages 107-108.) The youth minister and priest approve the night, albeit with suggestions for enhancing one or more of the segments. Finally, the core members make refinements and plan the specific details for each segment. Sometimes the outline goes back to the youth minister and priest for final approval.

On the day of the LIFE Night, the core members brief the rest of the core members on what is to take place and what their responsibilities are, set up the environment, and participate in a final rehearsal. This meeting should be concluded about one hour before the LIFE TEEN Mass so that the core members can be available to greet the teens on their way inside the church.

Music is also an important part of LIFE Nights, serving well as a transition time between Mass and the start of the session, and between the various segments.

Finally, having the priest present for as much of the LIFE Night as possible, especially for the closing prayer, communicates to the teens that he and the parish really love and care for them.

The Resource section of this book includes ten LIFE Night plans, some of which include reproducible blackline masters. A LIFE Night planning guide and evaluation forms are also included.

Other Types of Programming

Weekly Activities and Retreats

As the LIFE TEEN program grows, teens will look for more and more ways to delve deeply into their faith. Therefore, a regular weekly program of many kinds of activities and events should soon be part of the total youth ministry program.

If a youth ministry center or room is available, plan to have it open for regular hours during the week, offering things like Bible study, prayer group, a faith series, rap sessions, and drop-in times where teens can simply hang out. This will remind teens that the church grounds are a good and hospitable place to be.

Aim to have a weekend retreat every semester. A retreat is an invaluable tool for having the teens grow more deeply in touch with themselves, God, and their faith. Often, retreats are the times when teens make the commitment to live their lives for Christ. A two-night retreat is an ideal time span (see the Sample Weekend Retreat Plan on page 110). A weekend retreat offers time to provide most of the elements of total youth ministry, including a deepening of prayer, an increased sense of belonging among the teens, interaction with adult core members, and informal celebrations of Mass and the sacrament of reconciliation.

Part III

Resources
Best of LIFE Nights
Planning Guide/Evaluations
Weekend Retreat Sample Schedule

Best of LIFE Nights

The following pages present basic outlines of ten of the best LIFE Nights since the program's inception. These outlines are meant to be an aid to core members who are responsible for planning for individual LIFE Nights. They are not, however, meant to replace the necessary planning meetings that are required to make for a successful LIFE Night. Feel free to adapt each LIFE Night outline to fit your own particular situation. Also, several pages are marked for reproduction for use at LIFE Nights.

A Look at MTV

This is definitely one of those Nights that will always get a good response from teens. Music is a sacred cow to young people, and to say anything that might not reflect favorably on their favorite music group . . . well, let's just say you may be in for a heck of a battle. These teens were in diapers at the founding of MTV—Music Television—and this music has formed the soundtrack of their lives. Ready yourself for an interesting and important evening.

This LIFE Night will require several hours of research (divided among core members) that involves interviewing teens about the kind of music they like, listening to music, watching music videos, not only on MTV, but also on VH-1, Christian Video stations, and Country Music Television. Core group members must immerse themselves in the teen music culture in order to do the LIFE Night well. Watching hours and hours of music videos will affect you. Make sure to spend a great amount of time in prayer as you prepare for this night.

Goals

The purposes of this LIFE Night are to explore several of the messages in contemporary teen music and music videos, to give the teens a way to discern those messages, and to provide solid alternatives to objectionable music and music videos.

Atmosphere

This night has enough dynamite that it has the potential to explode at a moment's notice. Therefore, it is important to set the type of environment that will keep things calm. It is strongly recommended that you meet in a space that is as small as possible. Doing so helps to alleviate feelings of "us versus them," with the core members presenting the information being viewed only as "adults trying to tell us what to do." A smaller room eliminates the chance that some teens will argue or call out comments anonymously from a distance.

Also, set a holy atmosphere that will help to counteract some of the un-Christian messages of the music videos that will be shown. Set an environment in which the material can be viewed through the eyes of Jesus. Place several signs with relevant scripture quotations on the walls of the room. Another great touch is to keep a slide of Jesus (recommendation: a slide from Franco Zeferelli's *Jesus of Nazareth*) on a screen throughout the session. It is important for the teens to be reminded in this dramatic way of Jesus' presence as they discuss this topic.

Materials Needed

- VCR
- Big screen TV or video projector
- A great sound system to enhance the presentation of the music and music videos
- Prepared video with compilation of several music video clips popular among teens
- Several Christian music videos
- Signs with relevant scripture quotations
- Slide projector and slide image of Jesus
- Prepared video (black and white) chronicling a core group planning meeting for this LIFE Night
- White board or chalkboard

Gather

Jesus TV Skit/Song (about 5 minutes)

Begin the night by having a core member enter as a Video Jockey from "Jesus TV" and introduce a song that really gets the teens involved. Other core members might dress as a way-out rock band and lead the singing, perhaps even karaoke style. The purpose of the song is to get the teens fired up for the material that is to follow.

Planning Video (about 4 minutes)

At a planning meeting for this session, make a black and white video showing the core members sitting around a table talking about this "A Look at MTV" LIFE Night. The dialogue among the core members should focus on how concerned they are about some of the messages in music videos, yet how aware they are of how music permeates teen culture. The video should be produced in the style of the old "Dockers" commercials: the audio is constant, but the video shows a variety of close-ups of hands, planning sheets, faces from different angles, and so on. The video should be taken with a hand-held camera, accenting a bumpy, amateur look. The purpose of the video is to show the teens the genuine care and concern the core members have for them, especially related to this topic. Show it to the teens.

Audience Likes and Dislikes of MTV (about 3 minutes)

Have a core member interview the teens, asking them what they like and dislike about MTV programming, including some staples like "Beavis and Butthead." Also survey the teens on the kinds of music they like and why they like them. Finally, ask about what the teens dislike. Summarize and write some of the responses on the board.

Proclaim

How Would Jesus Look at MTV? (about 5 minutes)

This mini-teaching sets the stage for looking at several different music videos. Turn on the slide of Jesus and keep it on for the remainder of the Night. Use the list of likes and dislikes mentioned by the teens as a reference and as a transitional point. Ask the teens what they think Jesus would "like and dislike" about the kind of music that has been mentioned. Suggestion: Read the beatitudes (Matthew 5:3-12) and use them as a control list to match Jesus' teachings with the messages of the music.

Break

Viewing of Music Videos (about 30 minutes)

Show a variety of music videos which the core members have determined to be contradictory or questionable to Christian values. These can be grouped into separate areas, with each core member taking responsibility for the presentation on one or more area, for example: violence, materialism, the occult (Satanism), sex, and the degradation of women. The person responsible for each area must be well-versed in the message being portrayed and how it contradicts Christian values, as well as being able to provide some background on the performer(s) and a deciphering of the lyrics. To do this well requires a great deal of research, compiling many minutes from several videos and then editing them into a five-minute segment that depicts the theme assigned. After each presentation, the core member should read one of the scripture quotations that pertains to authentic Christian teaching. This segment is primarily for presentation of the videos and the core members' overviews. The teens will have a chance to respond next.

Large-Group Discussion (about 15 minutes)

After all the videos have been shown, allow the teens the chance to respond by offering their own comments or asking questions about the presentation. Focus the discussion on whether or not the teens agree with what was presented and the reasons they feel as they do. It is important to remind the teens that they should discern what they watch and listen to, and that they should keep Jesus and his teachings in mind as to what is appropriate or not.

Send

Positive Videos and Christian Music
(about 5 to 10 minutes)

Show short video clips of Christian music artists. It's possible that many teens have never heard Christian contemporary music. (**You!** magazine maintains an up-to-date list of Christian music artists.)

Prayer Time (about 10 minutes)

Gather everyone together, arms around each other, and allow for open, spontaneous prayer, including an appropriate song. Conclude with recitation of the Hail Mary and singing of "Ave Maria."

A History of the Mass

This is an educational LIFE Night, which at first glance seems boring because of the use of the word "history" in its title. On the contrary, this night can be totally fun, but also a learning experience about the history of the Eucharist.

When doing this Night, feel free to adapt the given scripts to meet your needs. The important thing is to remember to do skits that both teach the message and keep the teens' attention.

Goal

The goal is to give the teens an understanding of the history of the Mass in a way that is both enjoyable and educational. The teens will also leave the Night with a greater understanding of the liturgy, besides being able to trace key events in its historical development.

Atmosphere

The majority of the night is taken up with the presentation of eight skits, offering a chronological overview of the Mass from the Last Supper to present day. The atmosphere is very important to how these skits come off. They are presented in a Disneyland "Electric Light Parade" format, complete with parade music. Eight different groups of core members perform the skits and do so in a lighthearted and humorous way. Part of the humor may come in the costuming, for which the core member/actors are also responsible.

For the parade and performance, seat the teens in the center of a room and focus their attention on one staging area. All performers from the eight skits will march around the circle in order (Skit 1 to Skit 8) to parade music ("Electric Light Parade" or a suitable substitute) in one complete rotation until the actors for Skit 1 reach the staging area. The music stops and a light is turned on the staging area and off the rest of the space, darkening the actors who are not performing. After Skit 1 is performed, the music plays again and the actors make another rotation, stopping when the actors of Skit 2 reach the stage. This format is repeated until all the skits have been performed.

Materials Needed

- Spotlight or other suitable lighting for the staging area

- Copies of resource Mass 101 Pop Quiz (one for each teen)

- Pencils

- Copies of the reproducible resources for Skits 1 to 8

- Props and costuming for each skit

Gather
Mass I.Q. Test (about 5 to 10 minutes)

After the usual introductions, pass out the Mass 101 Pop Quiz and a pencil to every participant. Ask the teens to mark their answers to the nine multiple choice questions. After time for marking, tell the teens that if they pay careful attention to the rest of the material covered at the LIFE Night, they will have no doubts to which answers are correct.

Proclaim
Light Parade (about 45 minutes)

The core members planning this session should assign other core members roles in the eight skits well before the date of this LIFE Night. All core members are responsible for rehearsing their roles and for securing proper costuming and any other necessary scenery items. The resources at the end of this session provide a basic outline of the skits, including the information relevant to each period of history of the Mass. Allow at least five minutes for the presentation of each skit.

Break
Questions and Answers (about 20 minutes)

Invite a priest to present more information on the history of the Mass, especially related to the periods covered in the skits and on the quiz. Include time for the teens to ask questions of the priest related to the Mass. The "things to ponder" section at the end of the pop quiz includes questions that the teens can address to the priest.

Send
Closing/Prayer Time (about 10 minutes)

Lead the teens in a traditional Catholic prayer. Also allow for the spontaneous sharing of intercessory prayers. Conclude with the singing of "Profession of Faith" by Tom Booth.

Mass 101

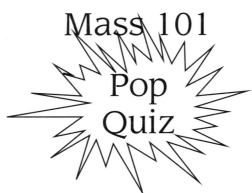

Pop Quiz

1. Who was the person who instituted the Eucharist?

    A. St. Peter

    B. Jesus Christ

    C. Pope John Paul II

    D. Monsignor Aloysius

2. True or False: Christians often have had to meet in secret in order to be able to celebrate the Eucharist.

    A. True

    B. False

3. Whose protest led to the start of the Protestant Reformation?

    A. John Calvin

    B. John Wycliffe

    C. Martin Luther

    D. Henry VIII

4. True or False: Any bread, including store-bought bread, can be used for Eucharist.

    A. True

    B. False

5. In the thirteenth century, the focal point of the Mass was:

    A. the elevation of the host.

    B. the alleluia.

    C. the Great Amen.

    D. the final blessing.

6. What is a change in the Mass that resulted from the Second Vatican Council?

    A. The priest turned around and faced the congregation.

    B. The altar was moved closer to the people.

    C. The priest was allowed to say Mass in the vernacular,

       the language of the people.

    D. All of the above

7. Who was the first person to declare Christianity the official religion of an entire nation?

    A. St. Peter

    B. Constantine

    C. Genghis Khan

    D. Henry VIII

8. The Catholic Church responded to the Protestant Reformation at:

    A. Vatican Council I.

    B. Vatican Council II.

    C. the Council of Trent.

    D. the Council of Nicaea.

Thoughts to ponder . . .

Why does the priest wear different color vestments throughout the year?

How come the first reading is usually from the Old Testament?

Why is the priest the only one to read the gospel?

What can a chalice be made of?

Why are there candles near the altar?

Why does the priest mix water with the wine?

Why do some people receive communion on the tongue?

History of the Mass/Skit 1
The Last Supper

Characters:

Jesus

John

James

Props:

Pillows	Cup
Candles	Wine
Bread	Costumes

Opening:

Jesus is preparing the Last Supper meal with James. John is away from the two, running a little late, and trying to find out where the meal is being held.

John (*running from teen to teen as if he were lost*):

Do you know where the Last Supper is being held? Do you? How about you?

Finally, John discovers James and Jesus in the Upper Room.

James: Listen, bro, you are always late. Don't you know this is the last meal we will ever share with Jesus?

John: I got tied up at the Temple. Then I got lost on Jerusalem Boulevard . . .

James: Well at least you're here, for Jesus' sake. John, have a seat over there. Jesus is about to begin.

Jesus: I have eagerly wanted to share this Passover meal with you before I suffer. For I tell you, I will not eat again until there is fulfillment in the kingdom of God. (Jesus takes the cup.) Take this and share it among yourselves. For I tell you, from this time on I shall not drink of the fruit of the vine until the kingdom of God comes. (Jesus takes the bread, blesses it, breaks it, and gives a piece to James and John.) This is my body, which will be given up for you. Do this in memory of me.

History of the Mass/Skit 2
Mass With St. Paul

Characters:

St. Paul

Husband

Wife

Props:

Pillows

Table

Loaf of bread

Unleavened bread

Cup

Wine

Paper Bag

Costumes

Opening:

St. Paul is celebrating the Eucharist at a family home in Corinth. A husband and wife who are neighbors arrive at the home to participate in the Eucharist. The wife has a paper bag containing a loaf of bread.

Paul *(greeting the neighbors with a hug)*:

Welcome, welcome. I see you brought bread for the meal.

Wife *(pulling out the loaf)*:

Yes, Paul. It is for our supper. I have also brought unleavened bread for Eucharist.

Husband *(taking the loaf)*:

We must share with our friends.

The husband, wife, and Paul break pieces of the loaf and distribute it randomly to the teens.

Paul *(motioning husband and wife back to stage)*:

Now, let us take the unleavened bread and wine and begin our prayer.

History of the Mass/Skit 3
The Secret Mass

Characters:
Table-Setter
First Guest
Second Guest

Props:
Pillows	Cup
Flashlights	Costumes
Unleavened bread	Candle

Opening:

Christianity was illegal in the Roman empire until the fourth century. This skit highlights the fact that Christians had to celebrate Mass in secret. The table-setter is setting a table for Mass in the candlelight. The first guest knocks at the door. Hearing the knock, the table-setter blows out the candle, takes a flashlight, and goes to open the door.

Table-Setter: Who's there?

First Guest *(panting noticeably)*:

It's me!

Table-Setter: Roses are red; violets are blue . . .

First Guest: . . . Jesus has risen and so will you.

Table-Setter *(opening the door and hurrying the First Guest inside)*:

Quick, before anyone sees you!

First Guest *(handing over the unleavened bread)*:
I brought it. The soldiers are everywhere.
I had to proceed more cautiously than ever before.

Table-Setter: Was anyone cast to the lions today?

First Guest: Yes, our friend Maria and her husband Thomas.
We must pray for their souls during Mass.
(The Second Guest knocks at the door. The First Guest goes to answer the door.) Roses are red, violets are blue . . .

Second Guest:	. . . sugar is sweet and so are you.
First Guest:	That's not it. Try again. Roses are red, violets are blue . . .
Second Guest:	. . . you look like a monkey and you smell like one too.
First Guest:	That's not right either. Away with you!
Second Guest:	Please let me in. I can see the soldiers coming. Please. I confess my belief in the Father, Son, and Holy Spirit. My name is Alex.
First Guest:	Okay, Alex. Come on in.

History of the Mass/Skit 4
Christianity Is Legalized

Characters:
>Constantine
>Protester (wearing hippie-type clothing)
>Supporter (wearing aristocratic clothing)
>Soldier

Props:
>Podium   Sword
>Picket signs   Costumes
>Scroll

Opening:

Here the Emperor Constantine is declaring that Christians will no longer be persecuted and, in fact, Christianity is to be the official religion of the empire. Constantine speaks from a podium as the protester circles around the stage holding a sign that says "Heck no, we won't go." Likewise, the supporter holds a picket sign, this one reading "Get some class, go to Mass!"

Constantine: Listen up everyone! I declare that beginning today, in 313 in the year of the Lord, Christianity is the official religion of the land. Christians are no longer to be persecuted. In fact, I expect every one to follow the rules of the Church. That means everyone is expected to attend Sunday Mass.

Protester *(shouting):*

Heck no, we won't go!

Constantine: What is all this confusion? My word is final. Must I escort you to Mass personally? *(Constantine leaves the podium and escorts the protester offstage.)*

History of the Mass/Skit 5
Sighting of the Eucharist

Characters:

Mother

Daughter

Props:

Bells

Drab clothing (e.g., long skirts, blouses, apron, headwear)

Opening:

The time period is approximately the eleventh century. Both characters are female. The scene begins with the sound of bells ringing offstage and the mother and daughter genuflecting and crossing themselves as they look in the distance over the heads of the audience.

Mother: That's my sixth Eucharist sighting this week. That certainly is more times than any of the other scrub maids have seen the Eucharist this week.

Daughter: Mother, why is it all you do is work, work, work? I never get to see you that much anymore. When I come home from begging in the streets, I have to let myself into the loft. Then I have to do all of the chores, like milking the goats and dumping the slop bucket. Why can't you be like other moms?

Mother: Other mothers don't have their husbands chasing after every crusade that comes along. Imagine freeing the Holy Land from those Turks! Since your father's gone, I had to take the job at the inn to support you. Besides, a little extra money at the church may get us a better seat when the holy Eucharist is raised.

Daughter: How come all we get to do is see the holy Eucharist? Why don't we ever get to receive holy communion? Sister Margaret got to.

Mother: She's a nun. Only nuns and the clergy get to receive the holy Eucharist regularly. If you really want to receive the Eucharist, I can see if we can get you into the convent.

Daughter: You mean not only will I get to receive the Eucharist, but I'll always have a good seat during the elevation? Sounds like a plan!

History of the Mass/Skit 6
Reformation

Characters:
Peasant Woman
Catholic 1
Catholic 2
Protestant 1
Protestant 2
Extra Crowd Members (if possible)

Props:
Two placards that say "Catholics"
Two placards that say "Protestants"

Opening:

The skit opens with the Catholics and Protestants faced off against each other, members of each group wearing the appropriate placards. There is a gap of about five feet between each group. As the scene opens, the Catholics are yelling, "More filling!" The Protestants are yelling, "Less filling!" As the yelling continues, the peasant woman walks down the road and stands in the space between the two groups.

Woman (*motioning to the two groups*):
Who are you and what are you arguing about?

Catholic 1: Well, we are Catholics and these others are Protestants who follow the teachings of this Luther fellow. They claim we have cluttered our churches and sanctuaries with statues and candles.

Protestant 1: Well isn't that true? How about a little simplicity?

Catholic 2: Well how about a bit of reverence for the teachings and traditions that have been in place from the apostles until now?

Protestant 2: No, the Bible is what's important.

Woman: Can't we all just get along?

Catholic 1: We will listen to you if you will to us.

Protestant 1: Okay, we will keep trying to work out our differences.

History of the Mass/Skit 7
Council of Trent

Characters:
  Newsboy
  First Man
  Second Man

Props:
  Newspaper
  Costumes

Opening:

The Council of Trent met in 1545 to 1548 to work out reforms and renewal within the Catholic Church. The scene opens with the newsboy holding up a newspaper and calling out the headlines.

Newsboy: Hear ye, hear ye, read all about it! Catholic Church leaders meet to plot reform and renewal.

First Man (*taking newspaper*):

  Hey, lad. I'll take one of those.

Newsboy: That will be six coins, sir.

First Man (*without paying*):

  Well, how about this? The Catholic bishops are meeting at the Council of Trent. They have made the liturgy of the Mass the same throughout the world.

Newsboy continues to stand with hand outstretched.

Second Man (*looking over First Man's shoulder at the newspaper*):

  What does it say about communion?

First Man: We will be able to receive communion more often, even every Sunday. And we should go to confession any time we commit a serious sin.

Second Man (*taking paper from First Man*):

  Let me see that.

Newsboy (*to Second Man*):

  Sir, that'll be six coins.

Second Man *(ignoring the Newsboy)*:

> It says they will start a system of seminaries in each diocese to train priests in Church theology.

The First Man and Second Man walk off the stage, keeping the newspaper. The Newsboy follows.

Newsboy: Hey there! Is somebody going to pay?

Second Man *(handing newspaper back to boy)*:

> Oh, sorry. Here's your paper back.

Newsboy: Oh, I hope you two catch the plague.

History of the Mass/Skit 8
The Second Vatican Council

Characters:

> Priest
> Choir Members (3)
> Construction Workers (3)

Props:

> Table to represent altar
> Hard hats
> Alb for priest
> Choir robes

Opening:

> *This skit is done very simply. The table is placed against the back of the stage. The priest faces the wall, away from the people, speaking in Latin. The choir simultaneously sings in Latin. The scene is interrupted by three construction workers.*

Construction Worker 1:   Excuse me. I've just come from Rome. The Pope and Second Vatican Council say that changes are to be made here.

Priest: Like what?

Construction Worker 1 motions to the crew. They move the altar near the front of the stage and gently lead the priest to face the people. Next, the crew heads to the choir, helping them out of their robes. The choir then moves to the front of the stage and leads the teens in a rousing contemporary liturgical song.

War And Peace

This experience is a definite LIFE Night winner for any group. This Night will get teens to respond to different situations that would be posed in the case of war. It brings with it great involvement among the teens. There will be a need for teens to discuss the events that take place, so make sure ample time (approximately one hour and fifteen minutes) is reserved to complete the activities planned. Allow for discussion, even if it gets fiery. A combination of patriotism mixed with Christian virtue is a dynamite mix.

Goals

The purpose of this session is to give the teens the opportunity to face choices they may need to make in the event that their nation is involved in a war. The teens will also gain a greater insight on the experience of war and the Catholic Church's stand on war.

Atmosphere

Armed forces recruitment posters should be set around the room. Posters naming the various choices the teens have once war "breaks out" should be hung prominently near various stations. The stations should be areas suitable for holding small-group discussions. One station depicts a cemetery; it should be decorated to represent the ultimate destruction of war. A facilitator directs the action and reads three scenarios that demand response from the teens. It is recommended that the facilitator dress the part of a television news anchor and be stationed at a news desk that can remain in the large-group area.

Materials Needed

- VCR and big screen television

- Video clips of various war scenes (may be taken from *Forrest Gump* or other movies)

- Armed Forces recruitment posters

- Printed posters with the names for the following stations: Army, Navy, Air Force, Marines, Coast Guard, Deferments, Conscientious Objectors, Non-Cooperative Status, Evader Status

- Copies of the resources for the Facilitator Script and Scenarios 1, 2, and 3

Gather

Short Video (about 3 to 5 minutes)

After the teens are settled, show a short video clip depicting various war scenes (for example, *Forrest Gump*) without offering comment.

Proclaim

Instructions and Briefing (about 8 minutes)

Set at a news desk, the facilitator announces the theme of the night and then reads or paraphrases from the World View resource. Following the presentation, the facilitator asks those who wish to enlist in one of the branches of the armed forces to move to the appropriate station. After those choices are made, the teens who are left are then drafted evenly into the armed forces or allowed to make one of the other choices listed on the posters: e.g., non-cooperative or deferment. Core members are assigned to each of these stations to help facilitate the small-group discussions.

Break

Small- and Large-Group Discussions (about 70 minutes)

After the groups are formed at the various stations, teens share why they chose to affiliate with the particular group or how they feel about being assigned to that group. Allow about five to ten minutes for small-group discussion. After the discussion, the teens return to the large-group area. The facilitator reads Scenario 1. After hearing this or the other scenarios, teens should be offered the chance to change groups. Small-group discussion on the issue then follows as the teens are asked to share their feelings about what they heard and how they imagine their reaction would be if they were actually confronted with this issue. A large-group roundup follows each small-group discussion time. In the large-group, teens should be given the opportunity to summarize their views shared in the small group. Also note that the scenarios indicate that certain groups of people are killed in action. These people should move to the cemetery as designated. Those in the cemetery can no longer participate in discussion. Proceed with this same format for Scenarios 2 and 3.

Send

Open Discussion and Summary of Church's Position on War (about 10 minutes)

This discussion should be a final review of the material covered and a short summary on the Church's position on war. If possible, this portion of the LIFE Night should be led by the priest.

Music and Prayer Time (about 10 minutes)

Call on the musician to lead a song with lyrics that speak of peace. Conclude the prayer time with the recitation of the Hail Mary and the singing of "Ave Maria."

World View
Facilitator Script

Script:

News flash! Iraqi troops have invaded Saudi Arabia and cut off all exportation of oil to the United States. Limited conflict breaks out between Saudi Arabia and Iraq. Allies of both sides are assisting. United States forces in the Middle East are monitoring an area over Saudi Arabia declared as a "no-fly zone."

At this point the teens should be given the opportunity to voluntarily enlist in one of the branches of the Armed Forces. Those who choose to do so should sit near the appropriate posters. All others remain in the large-group area where the facilitator continues.

Script:

Attention! Due to the down-sizing of the military forces within the past few years and the potential for a long-term war, Congress has reinstated the draft for both males and females. At this time, everyone must choose membership in one of the following groups:

Deferments. Members of this group may seek a deferment from the draft based on religious ministry, poor health, or personal or family hardship. If the deferment is granted, you do not have to be drafted.

Conscientious Objector. Once a person has been drafted, he or she may apply for C.O. status if there is a firm, fixed, and sincere objection by reason of religious training and belief to participate in war in any form, or the bearing of arms. Teens who choose this option, must be prepared to specify if they object to having any part in the military, or if they object only to bearing arms and would accept a non-combative role in the military.

Non-Cooperative Status. Those in this group refuse to be drafted or to seek any kind of deferment, or apply for conscientious objector status. These teens refuse to cooperate with the system in any way.

Draftee. Teens who allow themselves to be drafted are placed in one of the following branches and assigned one of two roles. Those who enlisted are also assigned one of the two roles:

> Army: Core members assign teens roles as Tank Commanders or Doctors.
>
> Navy: Core members assign roles as either Submarine Captains or Scientists.
>
> Air Force: Core members assign roles as either Bomber Pilots or Bomb Loaders.
>
> Marines: Core members assign roles as either an Infantry Lieutenants or Platoon Sergeants.
>
> Coast Guard: Core members assign roles as either Gun Ship Captains or Cooks.

All teens who choose to be drafted are assigned to the various Armed Forces branches first. Then the teens who choose deferments, conscientious objector status, or non-cooperative status are asked to report to the appropriate station. Once everyone is placed in a group and the teens in the Armed Forces are assigned a role, the core members facilitating each group should ask each person to tell why they chose the group they did or how they feel about being assigned to that group and/or role.

Scenario 1
Facilitator Script

All the teens are in the large-group area. After a roundup of the World View discussion, the facilitator presents the following material in news anchor style.

Script:

Late last week Iraqi troops shot down a United States fighter pilot enforcing the no-fly zone over Saudi Arabia. Congress has now declared war on Iraq. The fighting begins in the Middle East. Oil supplies are beginning to thin out in the United States. Iraq bombs Saudi Arabia and the neighboring country of Kuwait. United States military forces retaliate and all-out war begins. No attacks have taken place on United States soil.

Here is an update on the status of people who took or were assigned various roles.

Deferments. All members of this group were denied a deferment from the draft. If you were in this group, you may allow yourself to be drafted or become part of the non-cooperatives.

Conscientious Objectors. Your request was approved. You must now remain with the group in a non-military role or join one of the armed forces as a chaplain.

Non-Cooperative Status. You have fled the country to avoid the draft. You currently have little money and are experiencing difficulty finding a job in a foreign country. Your family members at home are being harassed to reveal your location.

Small-group sharing commences again with discussion of the latest developments. Also, facilitators delve more deeply into the moral correctness of each of the decisions for non-military participation: deferments, non-cooperative status, and conscientious objectors. Teens are asked to explain their choices more fully.

Scenario 2
Facilitator Script

All the teens are in the large-group area. After a round up of the Scenario 1 discussion, the facilitator presents the following material in news anchor style.

Script:

As the war progresses, many battles create heroes and heroic actions. Atrocities of war must also be confronted. Many casualties are also a reality. Here is some information about the roles of the various armed forces and some key military figures in the war.

Army. If you are a Tank Commander, you intercept enemy forces raiding and pillaging a friendly village. You are responsible for saving the life of a fellow service member and the lives of twenty innocent civilians. You are awarded the Bronze Star for heroism and bravery. You personally kill seven enemy soldiers to save the village. If you are an Army doctor, you set up a MASH unit, but due to the shortage of supplies you may only treat wounded American soldiers. The chaplains are in support of both the Tank Commanders and the Doctors. The Chaplain must also explain to the local Saudi Arabian civilians why they are not being treated by the doctor.

Navy. If you are the Submarine Captain, you are ordered to sink any enemy vessel encountered in the shipping lane you are patrolling in the Persian Gulf. A Destroyer with 110 men and seven women and a Transport ship with 60 men aboard are destroyed. If you are the Scientist, you are ordered to begin the design of a chemical warfare bomb capable of being delivered by the submarine. You are told this bomb will be used only to retaliate enemy use of similar warfare. The Chaplain counsels those involved on the moral issues of using chemical warfare.

Marines. Your platoon is led by unscrupulous officers. The Infantry Lieutenant is ordered on a search-and-destroy mission and personally kills seven men, four women, and two children. He also witnesses other killings and observes fellow soldiers while his superior officers condone this behavior. The Sergeant is ordered to lead a search-and-destroy mission and is encouraged not to deter the atrocities as a means of instilling fear into the enemy and sharpening the killer instinct of our own troops. The Chaplain is ordered to counsel those involved in the killings.

Air Force. The Fighter Pilot is ordered to drop bombs on populated areas where the enemy has set up command posts in civilian populations. If you are the Bomb Loader you are ordered to load the jets with Napalm bombs. Thousands of men, women, and children are killed or burned by the Napalm. The chaplain counsels those involved in these situations.

Coast Guard. If you are the Gunship Captain, you primarily patrol the water inlets surrounding the American base in Saudi Arabia. Usually you have no contact with the enemy. However, while on patrol, the Gunship Captain mistakes a refugee boat for the enemy and blows it up. Five men, three women, three children and various livestock are killed. The Cook is aboard the ship and assists in the attack. The Chaplain counsels the soldiers involved in the attack.

Small-group sharing commences again with discussion of the latest developments. Persons assigned to the roles mentioned above discuss their feelings about having been involved in these actions.

Scenario 3
Facilitator Script

All the teens are in the large-group area. After a roundup of the Scenario 1 discussion, the facilitator presents the following material in news anchor style.

Script:

Iraq begins attacking United States troops in Saudi Arabia with deadly chemical warfare. Our troops are getting too sick to fight and our hospitals cannot keep enough supplies in them to treat the soldiers. Iraqi terrorists have begun hijacking commercial planes in the United States. Many military units are returned to this country. We appear to be losing the war, and the President declares that it is time to take extreme measures. Some of the measures involve the following incidents:

Conscientious Objectors. You have now lost your C.O. status. You are now assigned to a military branch. *(Core members evenly assign the teens in the C.O. group to an armed forces group.)*

Non-Cooperative Status. You continue to have financial problems. Your family at home is forced to apply for government assistance. However, the government refuses support unless they tell your whereabouts. Their loyalty remains with you so now they are living on the streets. You decide to return. However, you decide to continue to protest the war. During a protest you accidentally kill ten American college students. You are arrested and convicted of murder and treason. You face the death penalty.

Chaplains. Your status remains in existence, however you are forced to relinquish your non-combatant status and carry weapons.

Army. The Tank Commander is order to use neutron bombs. The Doctor is ordered to carry a gun while treating casualties. As a result, the Doctor is called into a combat situation and personally kills three enemy soldiers.

Navy. If you are the Scientist, you develop a "germ warfare" bomb to use in retaliation. If you are the Submarine Captain, you trigger the explosion of the bomb that kills 360,000 Iraqis in one week. The deaths caused by this bomb are painful and prolonged in most cases.

Marines. All Marines are killed by poisonous gas. If you are in this group, proceed to the National Cemetery.

Air Force. The Bomb Loader loads an atomic bomb. The Fighter Pilot delivers the bomb on Iraq. Over six million people die within the week.

Coast Guard. During a pitched battle, the Gunship Captain is able to rescue a group of stranded soldiers who were fighting off the enemy from the shoreline. The Cook helps to feed the rescued soldiers.

Small-group sharing commences again with discussion of the latest developments. Persons assigned to the roles mentioned above discuss their feelings about having been involved in these actions. After small-group sharing, a debriefing of the entire experience takes place with all the teens present.

Spiritual Check-Up

This is a great LIFE Night to do when things seems to have gotten a little stale. This Night is done in the spirit of a doctor's check-up—complete with diagnosis and prescriptions. Teens are able to participate fully from start to finish. There will also be opportunity for core members to spend quality one-on-one time with teens. Go all-out on atmosphere and sharing. Positive results are guaranteed!

Goal

This session allows teens to be in touch with their own spirituality, particularly the things in their lives that are either bringing them closer to God or pulling them away.

Atmosphere

On one side of the meeting place, set up space to resemble a hospital. Have areas to represent an emergency room as well as separate areas for doctors to meet privately with patients. The "doctors" in this case are core members. They should dress accordingly in scrubs, masks, smocks, or white suits.

The teens will meet for spiritual consultation with "doctor" core members, either individually or in small groups. These meetings should be conducted in a warm and non-judgmental way. The teens should know they can be extremely honest.

Each separate consultation area should be labeled according to a spiritual diagnosis: good bill of health, spiritual exercise, radical surgery, and so on. The good bill of health and spiritual exercise areas are to be for group discussions. The radical surgery areas are for one-to-one discussions.

Materials Needed

- Medical clothing, clipboards, and folders for each core member

- A stretcher for the patient

- Other medical props—for example, stethoscopes, blood pressure gauges, eye charts, tongue depressors, rubber hammers

- For the skit, surgery items like an IV bag, operating light, ketchup (for blood), a rubber chicken, a wrapped candy bar, kitchen utensils for operating

- Copies of the resource Spiritual Check-Up (one for each participant)

Gather

Skit (about 10 minutes)

Done as a satiric take-off of the television show "ER," the skit introduces the LIFE Night's theme, pointing out the seriousness of maintaining spiritual health. Core group members act each of the roles.

The skit opens as two or three paramedics accompanied by doctors and nurses carry a patient into the emergency room area on a stretcher. Offstage, emergency room noises are heard in the background (sirens, hospital announcements over the P.A.).

A lead surgeon, along with a team of doctors, operates on the patient. One of the assistants provides up-to-the-minute reports on the patient's condition. The surgery proceeds with squirting blood (ketchup), simulated cutting using the kitchen utensils, removal of foreign objects (rubber chicken, candy bar). Well, you get the idea.

Despite the best of efforts, the patient flatlines and the staff uses the shock method (defibrillator) to bring him or her back to life. After a few tries, the patient is pronounced dead. The surgeon than addresses the teens, explaining the cause of death: *a poor spiritual condition.*

Proclaim

Teaching (about 4 minutes)

The surgeon then continues to explain briefly to the teens that they too can die spiritually, but that this death can only be fully prevented if the right steps are taken now. The surgeon then explains that all teens will have the opportunity for a free spiritual check-up. At this time, the doctors and nurses pass out a Spiritual Check-Up form to each teen.

Break

Individual "Doctor" Appointments
(about 30 minutes)

The teens take their forms to a core member ("doctor") and the two work together to fill them out. The teens should rate themselves as honestly as possible using the scale listed. The core members fill out the forms as the teens provide the information.

As the doctor goes through the issues, several accompanying actions work well. For example, they can grab the wrist to check the pulse while asking about Mass attendance, bang gently on the knee with a rubber hammer while asking about sexual activity, and so on. If time allows, the doctors should discuss some of the issues in more detail with the teens.

The doctor writes a prescription based on a totaling of the scores for each issue. The prescriptions are as follows:

0 to 10 Radical Surgery

11 to 16 Spiritual Exercise

17 to 21 Good Bill of Health

Spiritual Prescriptions Group Discussions
(about 15 minutes)

Each of the following group discussions should be led by at least two core members. For "Radical Surgery," one-on-one time is required. Use as many core members as necessary to facilitate these discussions. Take the following suggested topics as starting points and expand them with your groups. Teens will be coming in continuously as they finish their doctor appointments. Be aware of ways to involve everyone in the discussion.

Radical Surgery
Discuss the teen's low score. Focus on one or more issue. Look for ways to improve in these areas.

Spiritual Exercise
Discuss ways to fine-tune one's spiritual life, especially related to the areas on the Spiritual Check-Up.

Good Bill of Health
Discuss ways to perfect one's spirituality—for example, relevant spiritual reading suggestions may be given.

Send
Closing/Prayer Time (about 15 minutes)

Bring the teens all together in one room. When they are settled, a procession with the Blessed Sacrament begins along with the singing of any appropriate eucharistic song or song with a healing theme. Silent adoration takes place.

The prayer time ends with a recitation of the Hail Mary and the singing of the Ave Maria.

Spiritual Check-Up

Last Name _____ First Name_____

Doctor, please circle the number which coincides with the issue in question.
Use the following scale:

0 = Strong "No"

3 = Strong "Yes"

Spiritual Pulse:

Attending Weekly Mass   0   1   2   3

Reflexes:

Not Sexually Active   0   1   2   3

Temperature:

No Alcohol or Drug Use   0   1   2   3

Sight/Vision:

Reading Scripture/Religious Books   0   1   2   3

Breath:

Communicating Well With Family   0   1   2   3

Hearing:

Spending Time in Prayer   0   1   2   3

Tongue:

Not Gossiping or Swearing   0   1   2   3

0 to 10 Radical Surgery

11 to 16 Spiritual Exercise

17 to 21 Good Bill of Health

Prescription: _____

Doctor: _____

LIFE Olympics

This is a social LIFE "Night" that is actually to be held in the daylight. LIFE Olympics is an event that will have every teen talking. The events are not the typical athletic events, rather they are much more wacky and lots of fun. The way to make this really a successful event is to publicize it ahead of time, and then on the day of the event, reward teams even more for their enthusiasm than their results in any of the events. Make sure the core group members are in on this too. It is amazing the amount of excitement the core can pass on to the teens.

Goal

The goal of the session is to allow teens to enjoy themselves in a safe atmosphere, where they can participate in different events that don't really measure athletic skills as much as they are just plain fun! The LIFE Olympics should help all involved grow closer as a community, and provide core members an opportunity within an informal setting to meet and spend time with many different teens.

Atmosphere

The LIFE Olympics should create an environment that builds community and is safe, fun, and allows teens to go a little crazy! This event is best held in the summer since the weather is better and there is no school the day after. It usually is wise to charge a couple of dollars to participate, in order to help offset the costs. It is also recommended that you do the Olympic events on a Sunday afternoon, before Mass, as long as the teens have a chance to clean themselves up afterward. Then have the awards ceremony and a dance or party after Mass.

The events should be held on an open field (e.g., a football or baseball field), and the feeling of the Olympics should be in the air. A master of ceremonies should have a suitable sound system available so that announcements can be heard and everyone can be called together when necessary. Big signs marking each event and a scoreboard in a central place are musts. If you really want to go all out, have the core members make T-shirts for their teams ahead of time and have them wear them on the day of the Olympics. Try to have medals or other awards available for the winners. But also award those who show the most enthusiasm, win or lose.

The events suggested here are only some of the ones you may use.

Materials Needed

- Portable sound system

- Scoreboard (make this yourself)

- LIFE Games Scorecard and pencils for each team captain (core member)

- Open field (if the LIFE Olympics are to be held at night, it must have lights)

- Plenty of water, cups, and other refreshments

- Adhesive name tags

- Raw eggs (one per team)

- LIFE Olympics Things to Keep in Mind resource (one per team)

Gather

Registration (about 10 minutes)

As teens enter the event area, have a sign-in table where they can register. Each teen should be given a name tag that they must wear. Assign teens to teams so that there are about ten or twelve teens and one core member per team. (Teams with fewer members also work fine.) Core members serve as captains and can also be assigned to keep the score for their team. The LIFE Olympics Scorecard is included on page 89. Also give team captains the resource LIFE Olympics Things to Keep in Mind to be read to the teens on their teams. Assign team names using the animals listed in the first event. A reminder: Don't spend too much time registering and assigning teams. The games themselves are much more fun.

Proclaim

Opening Ceremonies (about 5 minutes)

This is just a quick rules-and-regulations time. The master of ceremonies should briefly explain how the teams will be scored for each event (finish and enthusiasm). For the first event (Animal Farm) all teams will compete together. After that, teams will be grouped with a partner team and have their events staggered so that the rotation will move more quickly. At this point, a raw egg should be given to a teen member of each team. Explain that the team will be given 15 bonus points for the safe return of the "egg mascot" at the end of all the events. Only teens can carry the egg. Other points for scoring are:

Winning Team (for each event) 10 Points

Losing Teams (for each event) 5 Points

Bonus "Spirit" Points (awarded randomly by the Master of Ceremonies and other unattached core members)

Assign unattached core members to monitor each event. They should judge and award scores to team captains who write them down. A representative of the team can also report the score to the person manning the scoreboard.

Break

The Events
(about 7 to 10 minutes for each event)

Animal Farm
Materials needed: blindfold for each teen

This event is held with all the teams in one space. Make sure each team is named for an animal that makes a distinctive sound (cow, chicken, donkey, cat, dog, monkey, duck, goose, lion, pig, rooster). Blindfold all teens. Then, on the MC's signal, all the teens make their respective team animal sounds in an attempt to link up with other team members. The first team to get all team members together is the winner. The core members help to determine the winner.

Human Wheelbarrow Race
Materials needed: orange cones to mark start and finish

This is a relay event. Two teammates, one on hands, the other holding the first person's legs, walk, run, or crawl as fast as they dare to a cone placed an appropriate distance (20 yards) away. Then they switch places with each other and head back, signaling the start for the next pair of teammates. (For competing teams with uneven pairs, one of the teams will have to have a pair race an extra time to keep things even.)

Three-People Race
Materials needed: cones, rope or strips of cloth (four strips for each group of three teens)

Like a three-legged race, the three-people race ties together the ankles and knees of three people. Only the outside legs of the two people on the ends are free. Team members are positioned equally at both ends of the course. The first three-person groups run, crawl, walk, and probably fall to the other side, tag the second group which proceeds back, tags the third group, and so on. All team members must participate. The team that finishes the course first (with all team members participating) is the winner.

Over-Under Balloon Pass
Materials needed: plenty of water balloons greased with cooking oil

All team members line up in a single file line, facing in one direction. The first person in line is given a big water balloon which happens to be greased with cooking oil. The first person passes it overhead to the person behind, who passes it under legs to the next person. The pattern than starts over. When the balloon reaches the end of the line, the person at the end sends it back, but this time reversing the over-under pattern. The first team to get the balloon all the way back to the front is the winner. If a team drops a balloon, they must start over at the beginning. If the balloon breaks, they are out of the game.

The Ultimate Relay
Materials needed: jump ropes, combination locks, one baby pool, clothes pins (one per team), coffee cans, baseball bats, and 10 or 15 cones

Each team should choose four teens for this event. The relay is set up in the following order:

First person jumps rope 10 times.

Second person unlocks a combination lock (combination provided).

Third person puts head in a baby pool of water and grabs clothes pin with teeth (no hands) and drops clothes pin into a can (using hands).

Fourth person runs to a baseball bat, puts forehead to top of bat, spins six revolutions around the bat, and then runs through a zig-zag course on the way to a finish line.

Make sure at least two teams can go at the same time.

Optional: You may wish to have each of the four team members do all four events.

Carrier Landings

Materials needed: A long sheet of plastic ("Slip and Slide"), several plastic ponchos (trash bags work), water and cooking oil

Four teens per team participate in this event. Prepare to get wet and messy. Each of the four players will have a chance to "land" three times. Here's how the event works:

Each player will take turns wearing a plastic poncho. On signal, one person at a time will run and dive head first on a long sheet of plastic (watered and greased). The goal is to come the closest to the end without going off the plastic. The person who comes the closest wins the event for his or her team.

Balloon Launch

Materials needed: water balloon launcher(s), lots of water balloons, two blankets or sheets

Three team members work a water balloon launcher, launching five balloons one at a time. The rest of the team stand about 100 feet away holding the sides of a blanket. As the balloons are launched, those holding the blanket attempt to catch them. The team that catches the most balloons on its blanket wins. Prepare for some people to get wet on this one.

Wheelbarrow Relay

Materials needed: at least two wheelbarrows, two hockey sticks, tennis balls, and cones

The teens work in pairs for this relay. One teen pushes the wheelbarrow while the other rides inside holding a hockey stick and pushing a tennis ball alongside as they go. When they reach the other side (marked by a cone), the two switch places and return to the start. Then the next pair takes over. Continue until all have participated. Make sure both teams have an even amount of pairs. The first team to finish is the winner.

Send

Closing Ceremonies (about 10 minutes)

Gather all the teams together and announce the winners, including winners of "spirit awards," and so on. All the first-place team members should get medals, but don't make that big a deal of it. Remember, the goal of the LIFE Olympics is to have fun and build community, not "win."

Prayer Time (about 10 minutes)

Close the Olympics by having the teens put their arms around one another and sing and pray. Recite the Hail Mary and sing the Ave Maria at the very end.

LIFE Olympics
Things to Keep in Mind
(for team captains to read to their teams)

1. Enthusiasm. It spreads, so let this be our attitude: to have fun within the rules.

2. Make sure all team members participate in the events. If some seem unwilling, give them a little extra nudge.

3. Dress for the event. If you are wearing something you don't want to get dirty, you should probably change now.

4. Drink plenty of water.

5. Keep the LIFE Olympics on schedule. If your team is not ready for an event, it may be disqualified.

6. Remember to show good sportsmanship. Anyone interfering with someone on another team will be disqualified.

7. Bring on the spirit. Remember, each team is able to receive spirit points for each event and additional points for bringing back the unbroken egg.

8. Have fun with your team and in the spirit of competition. Cheer on everyone! Enjoy!

LIFE Olympics

 *Team Scorecard*

Event	Team Score

Bonus Points

Total Points

Death and Dying

This is an "issue" LIFE Night that carries with it a huge impact. It combines personal testimony on the subject with a participatory exercise to create a deep experience that teens won't soon forget. Part of the Night includes testimony given by someone who has experienced the death of someone very close. If possible, ask a parent who has dealt with the death of a teen or a teen who has dealt with the death of a parent to speak with the group. Any testimony is bound to be powerful. If the speaker needs help in organizing the talk, share the five stages of grieving from this lesson plan and ask the person to relate these stages to his or her own experience. Understand that teenagers have an especially difficult time dealing with death because they rarely take the time to talk about it unless it hits them personally. This LIFE Night provides that chance.

Goal

This LIFE Night helps the teens to a greater understanding of death and dying, and the grieving process, from a Christian perspective.

Atmosphere

Create an environment that is conducive to deep and personal sharing. Make sure the space allows the teens to sit close to one another and to the guest speaker. If slides or videos are shown to accompany the speaker's presentation, make sure they can be easily seen from where the teens are sitting. However, during the Dying Exercise the teens should be able to sit at least six feet apart from one another, to avoid distractions. Arrange for instrumental music to play in the background during this time.

Materials Needed

- VCR or slide projector
- Big screen TV monitor or screen to show slides
- Microphone
- Small strips of paper (10 strips for each teen)
- Pencils

Gather

Opening Skit (about 5 minutes)

A teen and a core member improvise a skit that introduces the topic of death. The improvisation begins with the teen at home doing homework. The core member comes to the house for a short visit and then leaves. The scene flashes forward to a short time later. The phone rings and the teen answers to discover that the core member has been in a fatal accident a short distance from his or her house. The teen expresses to the audience his or her feelings of shock, denial, and anger for what has happened.

Choose a teen that is a natural actor. Include humor in the first part of the skit, especially representing the close relationship between the teen and core member. The ending of the skit should be extremely serious and powerful.

Proclaim

Personal Sharing (about 15 minutes)

Allow time for the presentation by the teen or parent who has experienced the loss of a loved one. The presentation may be even more meaningful if the teens knew or were familiar with the person who has died. To personalize the presentation, recommend that a short video or slide presentation of the deceased person's life be incorporated.

Teaching on the Grief Process (about 10 minutes)

Arrange for a core member or, if possible, a person who works in bereavement and grief ministry to give a short presentation on psychiatrist Elizabeth Kübler-Ross's five stages of grieving for understanding the dying process. They are:

1. Denial and isolation. At first, a person can't believe what has happened. This denial may lead to a feeling of isolation, and a blind hope that the whole experience will just go away.

2. Anger. This is a natural reaction and is triggered due to the resentment at being a victim. The person often takes out the anger on those close by: friends, family, doctors. Many times, the anger is directed against God.

3. Bargaining. The dying person or those close by attempt to gain leverage over the situation by praying, seeking better medical treatment, mending his or her ways. Promises like "If you let this person live, I will never sin again" are common.

4. Depression. The numbness, isolation, and anger of the earlier stages are now replaced with a sense of great loss.

5. Acceptance. This is a time of dealing with reality. The dying person may worry about what he or she will leave for the family. Acceptance also helps those connected with the dying to handle it in a constructive way. Hope is also an element of this stage. Everyone involved may see the good the person effects: for example, the death of a teen killed by a drunk driver may bring great awareness of this problem to his or her peers and community.

Break

Dying Exercise (about 20 minutes)

The teens take a pencil and ten small strips of paper and move to a spot where they can be at least six feet away from others. If possible, lower the lights and begin the instrumental background music. A core member should lead the exercise from the following script, reading slowly and pausing between sentences:

You haven't felt well lately, so you go to see your doctor. The doctor decides to run a few tests on you. When you get home you receive a call from the doctor telling you to stay where you are. Preliminary tests have shown that you have a disease that leaves your body without immunities.

Please take five of the sheets of paper and write down one material possession you would like to have with you as you spend this time alone.

You have also been advised to limit the number of people to see you, due to the concern that your immune system may not be able to fight off germs brought in by others. On the other five sheets, write down the names of five people that you would like to have with you during this time.

A week later, the doctor calls again to give you the final results of additional tests. You are told that the disease is in fact incurable and fatal. You have six months to live. As time progresses, you are no longer able to use many of the material possessions you have chosen. Tear up four of the five sheets with material possessions, leaving yourself with only the one thing you feel would be useful.

As the time of your death approaches, your medical aide has told you that you are only able to have two people visit you. Who would these be? Tear up the papers with the other three people's names.

Now, it is one hour before your death. Only one person can stay with you. Who will that be? Rip up the other sheet of paper.

You are a few moments away from death. What are you thinking about? Imagine what you would say to the person who is left with you. What would that person say to you? Think about your funeral. Who will be there? What will their reactions be to your death? How can your death have a positive impact on others?

Now, take your last breath and give up your soul.

Send

Large-Group Discussion (about 10 to 15 minutes)

A priest or core member leads a large-group follow-up to the exercise. Call on teens to share their feelings as they went through the process. Focus the discussion on what people teens had with them at the time of their death and their thoughts right before dying. Ask several different teens to share how they imagine their funeral, as well as the impact they imagine their lives to have had on others. Talk about Christian faith in the afterlife, as merited through the death and resurrection of Jesus Christ.

Prayer Time
(about 10 minutes)

The teens put their arms around each other for a time of spontaneous prayer intentions for the deceased of their families and parish, and especially for the family of the person who shared during the presentation. Sing John Michael Talbot's "Healer of My Soul" as part of the experience. Conclude with the recitation of the Hail Mary and the singing of the Ave Maria.

Note: Have core members, priests, and perhaps a counselor available after the LIFE Night for teens who wish to talk about issues related to death and dying.

Pro-LIFE Night

Welcome to a LIFE Night that will definitely spark some debate among teens. The abortion versus pro-life debate is a hot topic in all of society today. Obviously, the pro-life area includes more than just abortion. However, this Night focuses totally on the abortion issue, since most teenagers must deal with the reality of it. The session includes the actual burial of a baby casket at the end of the Night to symbolize and remember the hundreds of thousands of babies lost each year to abortion. This approach is strong, but it definitely helps to concretize the message to teens. Also, know that there are a number of ways to address the abortion topic. Several videos handle the topic well and can be used to replace one or more of the sections below. Consult a local Right to Life agency for recommendations. Whatever methods that are chosen, know that this LIFE Night is a must so that teens can lend a strong voice for life.

Goals

Goals here are to clearly present the Church's pro-life stance and to encourage teens who have had an abortion to reach out to the Church for healing.

Atmosphere

Teens are bound to have opinions on the opposite side from the Church's pro-life opinion. Be prepared to face those opinions strongly and concretely, but with respect. Also, some of the teens present may have had an abortion or know someone who has. Be careful not to offer condemnation, but rather the chance for healing and forgiveness. Project Rachel is the Church-sponsored National Office of Post Abortion Reconciliation and Healing and can be reached at 1-800-5WECARE. The symbolic funeral, burial procession, and prayer time at the end of the LIFE Night must be well planned. It is extremely helpful to have some of the teens involved in leadership roles for this time. The procession begins in the church and ends at a pre-dug hole somewhere nearby. All the participants should carry candles for the procession and keep them lit for the final prayer time.

Materials Needed

- Current information on the Church's position on abortion: including papal encyclicals. The subject is summarized well in *Sex, Love, and You* by Tom and Judy Lickona (Ave Maria Press). Also, note that **You!** magazine does a great job with providing up-to-date information on this subject in every issue.

- Candles with wax holders (one for each participant)

- A small wooden box to represent a baby casket

- Flowers (one for each teen to thrown onto the "grave")

- Shovel (to cover the casket with dirt after it is placed in the ground)

- Small white ribbons and pins (one for each teen)

- Copies of the resource, Pro-Life Scripture Passages (one for each participant)

Gather
Arguments and Rebuttals (about 5 minutes)

Present a debate on both sides of the abortion issue. Basically, the pro-abortion stance accepts abortions on demand as moral and legal, and advocates abortion as a possible solution to many problem pregnancies. Because of this, pro-abortionists are in favor of liberal abortion laws and present their arguments in terms of the mother having "rights" to control her own body. The pro-life position holds that abortion is morally wrong and should be legally wrong. Pro-lifers believe that abortion is the killing of an unborn baby and hold that no one should have the right to make that choice. The pro-life position is also concerned with a broad spectrum of life issues, including euthanasia, hunger, the death penalty, war, and poverty. Have one or more core members take the pro-abortion stance, and other core members the pro-life position. Specific points might involve the physical risks of abortion to the mother, the emotional risks to the mother and father, and the debate as to when life begins in the womb. The pro-life position should be presented in answer to each of the pro-abortion statements. Organize and rehearse the statements well in order to increase their impact.

Proclaim
Teaching (about 5 minutes)

As a transition, point out that every pro-abortion argument can be successfully rebutted, while every pro-life argument can be backed up by scripture, basic moral and human values, and by medical research. A core member should then clearly and concisely summarize the Church's position that life begins at conception and that having an abortion or supporting an abortion is likely an occasion of serious sin. Remember that sensitivity should be shown to teens who have had or know people who have had abortions; the church's love, mercy, and compassion should also be stressed. See the *Catechism of the Catholic Church*, 2270-2275, for a summary on the abortion issue. Use other appropriate references as well.

Break
Mini Question-and-Answer Rap Session
(about 15 minutes)

Include a priest, parent, doctor, and representative from a Right to Life agency in a panel discussion that allows all the teens to ask questions about abortion, including ethical, spiritual, and health-related issues. Teens usually have lots of questions to ask, so give them the opportunity to do so! Finish this section by letting them know some of the pro-life efforts being supported by teens in your area. Again, clearly emphasize the Church's position that being a Catholic and being pro-life go hand in hand.

Preview (about 5 minutes)

Explain what will transpire in the mock funeral and burial procession for an unborn child, as it has been arranged for your group. Give each teen a flower, a candle, and a wax holder and tell them to proceed to the church.

Funeral Procession and Burial (about 30 minutes)

Place the "casket" near the sanctuary. Have the teens be seated. Choose teens to read one or two of the scripture readings from the Pro-Life Scripture Passages resource. Ask a priest to share a short homily on the "right to life," especially regarding the unborn. A core member should offer a eulogy for Baby X, sharing some of the things this person will miss at various stages of life because of the decision made to have an abortion. Spontaneous prayer intentions follow, with all teens asked to share aloud or pray silently for their needs or the needs of someone they know.

Light the candles and darken the church. A dirge accompanies the recession of teens behind the casket to the area outside where the hole has been dug. Place the box in the hole. Offer one decade of the rosary (for example, Joyful Mystery, the Annunciation) near the hole. Allow each teen to blow out his or her candle, and throw one shovel of dirt on the hole. When the box is completely buried, the teens throw their flowers on the grave, join hands, and recite an Our Father.

Send

Final Song and Outreach (about 10 minutes)

The group sings an appropriate closing song, for example, "You Are Child" by P. Daniel Consiglio, or "Thank You for Having Me" by Michael John Poirer. Pass out white ribbons to all the teens and challenge them to wear them (especially to school) as a sign of their commitment to life in all forms. Also, give each teen a copy of the Pro-Life Scripture Passages resource.

Sing the Ave Maria to conclude the night.

It is advisable to have core members and a priest available to meet with individual teens at the conclusion of this LIFE Night. Also, refer as necessary any teen to the Project Rachel hotline number.

Pro-Life Scripture Passages

The following passages speak to the sanctity of life for the unborn. Read the passages. Pray for the lives of the unborn.

Psalm 139:13-15

Isaiah 49:1, 15-16

Jeremiah 1:4-10

Luke 1:39-44

Jesus as Healer

Jesus heals, both in the stories of the gospels and for people today. This LIFE Night recounts some of the examples of Jesus' healing in the gospels and allows teens the chance to pray for healing in their own lives and for those they know. The Send time is a time for the teens to offer some of their personal hurts to God and to receive the healing touch of the Church for their lives.

Goal

The goal is to help the teens come to know Jesus as healer, and to have the opportunity to offer the Lord something from their own lives that needs healing.

Atmosphere

The setting for the first part of the LIFE Night should be suitable for the presentation of short skits. The healing service that follows is best held in the sanctuary of the church or in a small chapel. During this time, the lights should be dimmed and all other distractions limited.

Materials Needed

- VCR
- Big screen TV monitor
- Videos to enhance the "teaching" presentation: for example, *Jesus of Nazareth* (the healing of the paralytic) and *Leap of Faith* (featuring Steve Martin)
- Small strips of paper (two or three strips for each teen)
- Pencils
- A basket to hold the strips of paper

Gather
Skits (about 10 to 15 minutes)

Core members develop three short skits portraying the healing power of Jesus. The skits should have a touch of humor while at the same time covering the basic content of the following gospel passages:

Skit 1   Jesus cures Simon's mother-in-law of her fever (Luke 4:38-39)
Skit 2   Jesus casts out a demon (Luke 8:26-39)
Skit 3   Jesus heals a paralytic and forgives him of his sins (Mark 2:1-12)

Proclaim
Teaching (about 15 to 20 minutes with videos)

Delve more deeply into the types of healing represented in each of the gospel passages. If possible, allow the teens the chance to follow along in their own bibles. For example, the curing of Simon's mother-in-law represents a threefold pattern of miracle stories recorded in the gospels: first, there is a problem (mother-in-law is sick); second, Jesus solves the problem (rebukes the fever); third, there is a response to the healing (mother-in-law gets up and waits on them). The teens may be directed to other gospel healing stories and asked to search for this pattern. Demonic healing is another type of healing performed by Jesus. Point out several examples in the gospels where the demons recognize Jesus and are afraid of his power. Ask the teens to name several demons in their own lives. Forgiveness accompanies many of Jesus' healings, as in the example of the paralytic. Ask the teens to guess why this might be so. Have them reflect on how forgiveness can help to heal hurts they have let fester with others or with themselves.

The showing of short video clips can help to enhance the presentation creatively. For example, in *Leap of Faith* a young boy is able to put down his crutches and walk. Steve Martin, who has faked all healings to this point, is as amazed as anyone that Jesus is able to do this. Also, *Jesus of Nazareth* includes many examples of Jesus' healings, including the healing of the paralytic man.

Break

Personal Sharing (about 5 to 10 minutes)

Arrange for a teen or core member to tell of a time he or she was healed physically, spiritually, and/or emotionally. The story may include an example of how forgiveness was a part of the healing equation.

Small-Group Discussion (about 10 minutes)

Related to the personal sharing example, have the teens meet with core members in small groups of six to eight and answer the following questions:

1. Can you talk about a time you were healed or healed another?

2. How did forgiveness play a part in your healing experience?

Send

Healing Experience (about 20 minutes)

Have the teens meet in the church sanctuary or other suitable place that has been chosen. Some reflective instrumental music should be played in the background. A priest should be present for this experience. When all are settled, ask the teens to think of something they would like to ask for healing from the Lord. Share several examples: drug or alcohol misuse, sexual activity, Satanism, abortion, lying, stealing, cheating. Make sure the teens know that they will not be identified with what they name. Tell them to write each thing they wished to be healed of on a separate strip of paper.

While the writing is taking place, a song with appropriate lyrics is sung (perhaps "Healer of My Soul" by John Michael Talbot, "We Believe in God" by Amy Grant, or "Reason to Live" by Ed Bolduc).

Allow a few minutes for writing. Then call the teens to come forward and place their papers in a basket. Next, a core member or a priest should lay their hands on the head of each teen and pray silently for healing of his or her needs.

Closing Prayer (about 5 minutes)

When all have brought their intentions forward and been prayed over, the priest lifts the basket in the air and offers a spontaneous prayer of healing for all the individual and larger intentions. A final verse of one of the healing songs is sung.

Conclude the Night with the recitation of the Hail Mary and singing of "Ave Maria."

The Ultimate Rock: The Pope

This LIFE Night is a total positive experience of the Catholic faith. Many non-Catholics and Catholics alike have misconceptions about the role and primacy of the pope. This session will allow the opportunity to clear up some of these misconceptions and to explain clearly the significance the bishop of Rome has always had in the Church. This LIFE Night was originally done in the week before World Youth Day in 1993. It will be easy for you to see how the teens left for Denver totally pumped up!

Goal

The aim is to help teens learn more about the history and traditions of the Church regarding the papacy as well as some biographical information about our current pope.

Atmosphere

The teens should be gathered in a place where they can easily view a big screen TV. The space should also be conducive to a "rally" where a person dressed as the pope can be paraded around the room to shouts and cheers. Small-group discussion (groups of four) is also part of the Night. Ample space should be reserved for the small groups to meet in areas well apart from one another and yet be able to easily return to the main meeting space for large-group roundup.

Materials Needed

- VCR
- Big screen TV monitor
- A video that covers the life and times of Pope John Paul II, for example: *Pope John Paul II: Statesman of Faith* (A&E documentary) or *The Journey to America* (EWTN, the Pope's 1995 trip to America)
- The video *Life to the Fullest* (Catholic Life Incorporated, World Youth Day 1993)
- Theme music from *Rocky*
- Cassette or CD player
- Current popular teen music that can be adapted with lyrics that speak of the pope (for example, The Spin Doctors' "Two Princes" redone with the lyrics "one pope")
- Costuming for the "pope"
- Costuming for the "secret service"
- A red wagon for the "popemobile"

Gather
Pep Rally Welcoming the "Pope" (about 5 minutes)

After the teens have arrived, let them know that this LIFE Night is a time for them to show their support for the Holy Father. Tell them that no expense has been spared and that the Holy Father has been brought to your parish especially to see them. At this point, strike up the *Rocky* theme and have the core member dressed as the pope led into the room on a "popemobile" (a red wagon), waving to the teens as he is pulled around the room surrounded by core members dressed as secret service agents. While this procession is going on, another core member leads the teens in cheers for the pope ("Long live the pope" and so on). Once the popemobile makes its way around the room, allow it to disappear out the door while the chants continue.

Proclaim
Teaching on the Papacy (about 5 minutes)

A core member prepares and presents a brief teaching on the papacy, including the following points:

- The apostolic nature of the Church, beginning with Jesus' giving of teaching authority to Peter (see Matthew 16:18-19). Because Peter was the bishop of the first community of Christians in Rome and because he died there, the succeeding bishops in Rome have always had a position of primacy in the Church.

- Papal infallibility. The pope speaks infallibly when he teaches *ex cathedra*, that is, "from the chair" of Saint Peter. To be an ex cathedra teaching, it must be a teaching by the pope in his role as visible head of the whole Church, a teaching addressed to all Catholics, a definitive statement on faith or morals, and an unchangeable teaching in which the pope has used his full authority. Papal infallibility was declared officially at the First Vatican Council in 1850. The last time a teaching was issued ex cathedra was in 1950 when Pope Pius XII taught that Mary was assumed body and soul into heaven.

Background on the Life of Pope John Paul (about 5 minutes)

A core member prepares and presents a brief summary of the life of Pope John Paul II, including the religious experience of his teenage years through to the most recent events of his life.

Video Presentation (about 15 minutes)

Pope John Paul II has had a tremendous effect on the youth of an entire generation. Exploring his life and message in more detail is certainly worthy of the time. The best documentary on his life is the Arts and Entertainment presentation, *Pope John Paul II: Statesman of Faith*. Choose and play a ten- to fifteen-minute segment of the video that summarizes and expands on some of the material presented on his life. *The Journey to America* is another option. It is a video that covers the 1995 trip the Pope made to America.

Break

Small-Group Discussion (about 10 minutes)

Have the teens meet in groups of four with one core member serving as facilitator for each small group. Provide the following questions for discussion:

1. How would you answer a non-Catholic friend who says that "Catholics blindly follow the pope"?

2. If you met the pope face-to-face, what would you ask him?

World Youth Day Video (about 15 minutes)

The video *Life to the Fullest* captures the experience of World Youth Day in Denver in 1993. Play it in its entirety.

Large-Group Sharing (about 10 minutes)

If any core members attended World Youth Day or have been in the presence of the pope at another time and place, have them briefly share their experiences following the playing of the video. Or, have core members share their thoughts and reflections on what "being Catholic" means to them.

Send

Prayer Time (about 10 minutes)

Pray a litany of the saints (for example, "St. Michael, pray for us") allowing the teens to voice out loud a saint they want to pray for them. After the litany, sing an appropriate song (such as "We Are One Body" by R. Scallon).

Song and Dance (about 5 minutes)

End the night with a rousing time of song, accompanied by some simply choreographed dance moves, in rally format. The core member dressed as pope can return to lead the rally. It is recommended that you take a song currently popular with the teens and rework the lyrics so that it speaks a positive message about the pope.

Timmy Awards
(insert the your parish name for "Timmy")

This is one of those fun social LIFE Nights that you can do every year. This Night allows teens to use their creativity, talent, and acting ability to write, direct, and produce their very own five-minute feature, commercial, or music video. Volunteering groups of up to five teens are given two weeks to create their "masterpiece" with no professional help, but under the direction of an assigned core member. Official registration to enter the contest should take place at least three weeks in advance of the scheduled Night. Consider offering suitable prizes to the winning teams to encourage more teens to participate. Assign core members to registered groups to make sure they complete their videos on time. Give each group a copy of the resource, Video Awards Rules and Regulations. On the LIFE Night itself, each video is introduced with fanfare and played for the audience. Live acts should be arranged to be performed between the showing of the videos (e.g., teens as comedians, piano players, dancers, gymnasts, etc.). All teens present in the audience serve as judges, rating each video according to the scale given on the scorecard.

Goal

The goal here is to allow teens to participate in a social LIFE Night that is hip on technology, fun, has all the atmosphere of the Academy Awards, and provides plenty of opportunities for them to get involved.

Atmosphere

The room should have a staging area, with rows of chairs facing the stage. On the stage, very visible to all, is the big screen TV or video projector. A backdrop on the stage should feature the name of the parish and the current year of this awards show. Provide a podium and microphone for the master of ceremonies. Add any other decorations to the stage that will add "class" to your LIFE Night awards show, such as Christmas lights, foil, or streamers.

Materials Needed

- VCR
- Big screen TV or video projector
- Microphone
- Copies of the resource Video Awards Rules and Regulations (one for each teen involved in making a video)
- Copies of the resource Award Night Scorecard (one for each teen in the audience)
- Pencils
- Spotlight (if possible)
- CD player or more advanced sound system
- Recordings of several songs to enhance the presentation
- Snare drum
- Video cameras (as needed by teens participating in this activity)

Gather

Understand that the flow of this LIFE Night will vary depending on the number and kind of videos and live acts you have.

Live Opening Act (about 5 minutes)

Play a recording of "That's Entertainment" or a similar song as the teens enter the room. You may want to have two core members imitate Fred Astaire and Ginger Rogers and dance and lip sync to the show tune of their choice. Or you could have several male chorus members come out in a "chorus line," doing synchronized kicks. (Of course, this act must be choreographed and rehearsed ahead of time.)

Grand Entrance of the MC (about 2 minutes)

Other core members, formally dressed, carry the master of ceremonies (also a core member or extroverted but focused teen) onto the stage, accompanied by loud and bold music.

Proclaim

Welcome from the MC (about 5 minutes)

The master of ceremonies welcomes the audience and gives the rules and format for the night. The Award Night Scorecards and pencils are handed out and explained at this time. If possible, the MC also gives a mini-monologue, Leno/Letterman style.

Videos (about 12 minutes)

The MC then introduces the first two videos (grouped by theme), which are then played back to back. The audience writes the names of the videos on the scorecards and grades them as they wish.

Live Act (about 5 minutes)

A teen does a lip sync, karaoke-style, of a popular song. If possible, simple dance steps can be incorporated into the performance to encourage audience participation.

More Videos (about 18 minutes)

The MC introduces three more videos (grouped by theme), which are then played and scored.

Live Act (about 5 minutes)

A short, stand-up comedy routine works well at this time.

More Videos (time will vary)

The last group of videos (maximum of four) are introduced and played.

Intermission (about 10 minutes)

After all the videos are shown, collect and tabulate the scorecards. During the intermission time, provide some appealing snacks and drinks for the teens to enjoy.

Last Year's Winner (about 5 minutes)

If you've done this before, use the time after the intermission to show last year's winning video.

Send

Announcement of Winners (about 5 minutes)

Complete with a drum roll, the MC announces the winning videos, beginning with the third-place winner.

Prayer Time (about 10 minutes)

Gather everyone, arm in arm, and have the priest lead a prayer experience. Recite the Hail Mary and sing the Ave Maria as a closing.

Mass Exodus and Clean-Up

Have the teens help with the clean-up so that the core members won't be there until midnight! And, yes, have some appealing teen music playing during this time.

Video Awards
Rules and Regulations

1. Your video production may be a music video, commercial spoof, or short-subject presentation no longer than five minutes in length.

2. You may have up to but not more than five teens in your group. A core member will be assigned to your group to assist you and to remind you of deadlines.

3. The final version of your video must be turned in to the youth minister one day before the LIFE Night. It will be reviewed before the LIFE Night Awards. If there is any offensive material in the video it will not be shown.

4. We will try to put you in touch with people who have video cameras to use. Of course, it is preferable if someone in your group supplies their own video camera for use on this project.

5. If you have any questions or need help, all you need to do is ask!

Award Night Scorecard

Directions: Write the name of each video as it is announced. Then rate the four areas based on the scale below. Add and write in the total for each video.

Please rate each video using 10 as the maximum score for each category. Then add the categories and place the totals in the appropriate column. To help speed the tabulator, please circle your highest total score.

HIGHEST   LOWEST
10  0

Video	Originality	Plot	Production	Acting	Total

Permission to reprint granted for use with this book and the LIFE TEEN program.

LIFE Night
Planning Guide

LIFE Night Date:

LIFE Night Title:

LIFE Night Team:

Educational Night____   **Issue Night____**   **Social Night____**

Goal for LIFE Night:

Atmosphere for LIFE Night/Set-Up:

Five-Minute Frenzy/Brainstorming:

LIFE Night
Planning Guide
(continued)

Be specific with amount of time allowed for each segment. Also include who will lead each segment and the basic content of the segment.

GATHER (Hospitality, Welcome, Introduction of Topic)

PROCLAIM (Teaching, Witnessing)

BREAK (Experience, Sharing, Depth, Groups)

SEND (Prayer, Inspiration, Concrete Actions)

PLUG-IN TO LIFE

Evaluations

This resource is for core members responsible for planning and leading a LIFE Night. Cut on the dashed lines. Distribute to core members at the appropriate times.

Questions to answer after planning of LIFE Night:

LIFE Night title:

LIFE Night date:

What is specifically creative about this LIFE Night and will appeal to teens?

What is specifically CATHOLIC about this LIFE Night?

What kind of potential is there to have "depth" experiences at this LIFE Night?

Other comments:

Questions to answer after the LIFE Night:

LIFE Night title:

LIFE Night date:

What did the teens say about the Night?

What elements do you feel worked?

What elements do you feel did not work?

How are the teens closer to Christ and the Church because of this LIFE Night?

Other Comments:

Weekend Retreat
Sample Schedule

The following schedule provides a skeletal outline of a weekend retreat. It is recommended that you choose a retreat theme (examples might be "New Life," "Commitment," or "Reconciliation") and plan presentations and follow-up exercises to fit the theme. Remember to be creative! Also, make sure to allow time for the sacrament of reconciliation and final, uplifting Sunday Eucharist back in your home parish.

The notes for the four main sessions below are taken from a LIFE TEEN retreat called "Go Light Your World," dealing with the subjects of light and darkness and sin and forgiveness.

Friday p.m.

5:00	Meet at Church
5:30	Departure for Retreat Site
7:00	Arrive at Retreat Center
7:30	Dinner
8:30	Introduction/Prayer/Theme Song
9:00	Session 1

What Is Darkness? . . . Sin!

A Gather, Proclaim, Break, Send presentation that names the darkness of the world as sin, tells where it comes from (Satan) and discusses ways to expose sin so that it can be extinguished.

10:30	Snack and Break
11:30	Night Prayer
12:00	Lights Out

Saturday a.m.

8:30	Breakfast
9:30	Warm-up Exercise
10:00	Session 2

How Do I Add to the Darkness? How Do I Add to the Light?

A Gather, Proclaim, Break, Send presentation that stresses the need for maintaining a committed relationship with Jesus in order to make it through the darkness of the world. This is the bond that is first given to Christians at baptism, and strengthened through the participation in prayer, scripture study, and the sacraments.

Saturday p.m.

12:00	Lunch and Long Break
2:30	Rap Session for Boys/Sacrament of Reconciliation for Girls
4:30	Sacrament of Reconciliation for Boys/Rap Session for Girls

5:30	Break
6:00	Dinner
7:30	Session 3

Jesus Is the Light of the World

A Gather, Proclaim, Break, Send presentation that shows how Jesus is a light that no darkness can extinguish. The teaching for this session is based on several scripture passages, including: 1 John 1:5-7; John 1:4-5; John 9; and Mark 4:21.

9:00	Break
9:30	Celebration of Holy Mass
11:00	Free Time
11:45	Night Prayer
12:00	Lights Out

Sunday a.m.

8:30	Breakfast
9:30	Morning Meditation/Warm-Up
9:45	Session 4

What Are Some Ways That We Can Be Light to the World?

A Gather, Proclaim, Break, Send session based on Jesus' call to serve the "least ones." Included in the Proclaim teaching may be a lesson based on the life and mission of Mother Teresa.

11:15	Clean-up/Packing

Sunday p.m.

12:15	Lunch
1:00	Evaluation
	Sharing/Closing Prayer
1:45	Leave Retreat Center
3:15	Arrive at Church/Light Supper
5:00	Teen Mass

MAY 2 6 2005